At a time in history when the Max Myers brings an importar us. This is not just a book abou~~ ~~~~~~~~ip princi-ples. Max reminds us that the most important aspect of leadership is reliance on the Holy Spirit. We must have Spirit-directed leadership in this crucial hour. I have watched Max lead, and I like where he is going...because his passion is following the cloud of God's presence.

—J. LEE GRADY, EDITOR
CHARISMA MAGAZINE

I love sitting at the feet of seasoned leaders. They have so much to impart and I have so much to glean. Max Myers is one of those seasoned leaders. You will be blessed as you learn deep lessons from his many years of experience and insight. *The Tail That Wags the Dog* will truly give you food for thought and will challenge you to go higher—much higher.

—PATRICIA KING
XPMEDIA.COM

Sonny,

Bless You as you move the Kingdom forward through intercession and activation. May your leadership in this arena be amplified by the power of His Spirit. I have every confidence that your most effective years are ahead of you.

Bless You,

Max

the
TAIL
that
WAGS
the
DOG

MAX J. MYERS

CREATION
HOUSE
A STRANG COMPANY

THE TAIL THAT WAGS THE DOG by Max J. Myers
Published by Creation House
A Strang Company
600 Rinehart Road
Lake Mary, Florida 32746
www.strangbookgroup.com

Unless otherwise noted, all Scripture quotations are from the New American Standard Bible—Updated Edition, Copyright © 1960, 1962, 1963, 1968, 1971, 1972, 1973, 1975, 1977, 1995 by The Lockman Foundation. Used by permission. (www.Lockman.org)

Scripture quotations marked NIV are from the Holy Bible, New International Version of the Bible. Copyright © 1973, 1978, 1984, International Bible Society. Used by permission.

Design Director: Bill Johnson

Cover design by Justin Evans

Copyright © 2009 by Max J. Myers
All rights reserved

Library of Congress Control Number: 2009932991
International Standard Book Number: 978-1-59979-913-1

First Edition

09 10 11 12 13 — 9 8 7 6 5 4 3 2 1
Printed in the United States of America

CONTENTS

Dedication

I am honored to dedicate this book to my wife, Nina, and my children, Renae and Jeff. You have lived this journey of leading God's people with me every step of the way. May your sacrifices and tears of those years be like rain on the new church that is about to arise. Couldn't have gotten here without you. Your spirit is alive within these pages.

■ ■ ■

Special Thanks

Special thanks to Doris Schroeder for all of her editing and formatting assistance. Special thanks also to Neil and Rita Swanson, Dale and Doris Schroeder, and Joel and Roxann Schwarze for giving yourselves to Nina and me unconditionally through this leadership journey as great friends. May the seeds of your friendship be blessed with supernatural fruit in the years to come.

INTRODUCTION

FOR AS LONG as I can remember, I have been familiar with the phrase "the tail was wagging the dog." It makes an interesting visual picture when you give your imagination a chance to put the phrase into action. Of course, it is physically impossible in the natural, but whoever first coined the phrase knew that everyone who heard it would get the point.

"The tail was wagging the dog" is a blatant characterization of a situation where roles of authority have been reversed. In the natural, the dog's tail has been attached to the body of the dog and is responsive to the direction and will of the dog. The phrase "the tail was wagging the dog" is descriptive of a scenario where a smaller entity that was meant to respond to a larger entity has now become the controlling force.

I propose to you that this is precisely what has happened to the church. The body of the dog represents the kingdom of God. It is where everything exists and works together as a powerful magnificent unit. It is where everything was created and from which it originates. It is where all the power and potential of an incredible God exists.

The tail is the church. It was meant to reflect the heart and attitude of the kingdom of God. When you watch the tail, you know what is happening with a dog. Like the tail of a dog, the church was birthed in the heart of God to follow His leading and respond to His direction as an inspiration to others.

Over time, God's people decided that they could do a better job at expressing and moving the kingdom than God could.

The church built human structure, programs, and systems that would give it a basis of influence. It began to dictate to God what He could and couldn't do. The church has decided how the kingdom will be expressed, and it has basically let God know that it is quite capable of handling things on its own, thank you. Of course no one in the church has come right out and said it like that, but those choices are evident through the fruit and in how leadership is developed.

If we, as the church, choose to continue to live under the authority of the tail instead of under the authority of God Himself, there is no way that we will ever see our potential realized. We weren't made to function this way. God is supposed to be the absolute resource and authority in all things.

God is looking for a generation who will let Him be in charge. He is looking for people who will restore the original pattern of the church's relationship of dependence and trust in Him. He is looking for people who are hungry and ready for the supernatural and tired of living at the level of the natural. He is looking for pastors and leaders who are tired of natural leadership and are ready to step into supernatural leadership. Without a doubt, right now, God is looking at you.

PART I

THE PRESENT LANDSCAPE

Chapter 1
WE'RE IN THIS TOGETHER

I T WAS A dark and stormy night.

Isn't that the way all great mystery books begin? Well, then, it's the way this book should begin, because we are about to track down a great leadership mystery. Many of you would love for me to just tell you what the mystery is and give you the solution over the next few pages. That's not going to happen. You see, this great leadership mystery can't be solved with just the rational mind. Yes, of course, you are going to have to use your mind, and our solution must be rational, but it's going to take more than that. It is going to take your heart. Give me your intellect, your reason, *and* your heart for the hours and days that you read through these pages. You will never be the same. Why? How? There you go, wanting the answers in the first paragraph! Just take a deep sigh and breathe up a "What am I getting myself into?" prayer. Now join me as a fellow sojourner in this land called "leadership" in the body of Christ. You will never be the same.

Many of you like me are wearing or have worn a title that comes along with leadership responsibility. Though in different environments the titles can vary, what most of us are called is "pastor." If you are not a pastor or in some similar place of leadership, don't disqualify yourself from reading the pages that lie ahead. You will find the unraveling of this great leadership mystery to be fascinating. In fact, your encounter with these truths will cause you to be able to step into kingdom arenas that, at best to date, you could have only dreamed of. Come, let's begin this journey together.

It was a dark and stormy night. If you have been attempting to lead God's people for any length of time, you have experienced the reality of that phrase. It is the darkness of local church leadership that surprises us the most. How could we have ever foreseen the seasons of trying to find the answer to questions like:

- What is my position on this situation supposed to be?

- How am I supposed to handle this crazy dilemma?

- Where can I get help to guide me through this?

- What are the possible outcomes of my decisions here?

- If this is such a great calling, then why do I feel so frustrated?

Wading through the demands of church leadership can be a very dark place at times. We feel as though we're lost without a compass and the darkness is so real we can reach out and touch it. Has it ever struck you as being odd that while we are searching through the darkness for answers there is always someone in our church who knows exactly what we should be doing? Church leadership is such an unusual arena.

Of course, the darkness of church leadership can be difficult to navigate, but what about those occasional storms? Don't you love it?

- The first situation brings in lightning that shocks everyone.

- The second situation brings into the atmosphere a wind that carries a stench in and families out.

- The third situation comes in like an arctic blast. The snow causes all forward progress to come to a halt, and everyone hunkers down, waiting for it to blow over.

If you have been involved in church leadership for any length of time, you know what I mean when I say, "It was a dark and stormy night." On the other hand, something inside tells us that it shouldn't be that way. Surely shepherding God's flock and moving them into greener pastures was meant to be different than this.

I remember the years of pastoring my first church in Morris, Illinois. The first three years we were there, I would have been lucky to have gotten the congregation to follow me to the coffee pot, let alone into an unseen spiritual kingdom. It was obvious to me that I had a lot to learn. The positive side of leading in darkness is that it motivates you to seek for a light. There's nothing like not being able to see where you are, where you are going, or what is happening around you, to cause you to long for some light on your situation. It is the seasons of darkness that begin to motivate you to think "How did I get here?" and "How can I avoid coming here again?" So many times we crank the sequence of events backwards, passionately looking for that event, reaction, or decision that led to the mess in which we find ourselves.

This leadership road has been well-traveled by those who have gone before us. Over the generations we have been blessed by great men and women of God who have shared with us the wisdom of their success. They have given us keys to live by as we shepherd God's great people. Each of us who has ever wanted to be successful in kingdom ministry has searched for the wisdom of others to guide us in this wonderful yet challenging life leadership journey.

There is no way that we can encapsulate the vast amount of their combined wisdom into a few brief pages. In order for us to get to where we are going in the chapters ahead though, we do need to take some time to be reminded of what they have brought to the table.

Oswald Sanders, in his book *Spiritual Leadership*, brings these lessons to us:[1]

- A leader is a person who has learned to obey a discipline imposed from without, and has then taken on a more rigorous discipline from within. Those who rebel against authority and scorn self-discipline, who shirk the rigors and turn from the sacrifices, do not qualify to lead.

- A leader shows patience by not running too far ahead of his followers and thus discouraging them. While keeping ahead, he stays near enough for them to keep him in sight and hear his call forward. He is not so strong that he cannot show a strengthening sympathy for the weakness of his fellows.

- The leader must be a person who, while welcoming the friendship and support of all who offer it, has sufficient inner resources to stand alone—even in the face of stiff opposition to have "no one but God."

- The leader must either initiate plans for progress or recognize the worthy plans of others. He must remain in front, giving guidance and direction to those behind. He does not wait for things to happen, but makes them happen.

■ Failing to delegate, the leader is caught in a morass of secondary detail; it overburdens him and diverts his attention from primary tasks. People under him do not achieve their own potential. In some cases, insisting on doing a job oneself is a result of simple conceit.

Bill Hybels, in his book *Courageous Leadership*, shares this leadership wisdom and experience from his years at Willow Creek:[2]

■ Ten years ago I...wrote these words: "The local church is the hope of the world and its future rests primarily in the hands of its leaders." For the first time, I realized that from a human perspective the outcome of the redemptive drama being played out on planet Earth will be determined by how well church leaders lead.

■ Jesus was not the least bit laissez-faire about building the kingdom. His passion for the lost and his love for the church were so strong that He took His Father's business all the way to the cross....I think He expects today's church leaders to put their best efforts into building prevailing churches.

■ Vision increases energy and moves people into action....It puts the match to the fuel that most people carry around in their hearts and yearn to have ignited. But we leaders must keep striking that match by painting compelling kingdom pictures.

■ The first step in building a dream team is to define the purpose of the team....Now whenever pastors tell me they're going to put together a leadership team my reflex is to ask a few clarifying questions. "What kind of leadership team? What will be its purpose? Will it be to help you with your preaching? To create church policy? To discipline wayward church members? To buy property and build buildings?" I ask these questions because I know that these widely different tasks may well require people with widely different gifts, skills, and expertise.

■ Certain leadership styles fit better than others with specific kingdom needs. I am increasingly convinced that highly effective leaders often have impact not only because they are highly gifted but also because their leadership styles mesh perfectly with specific ministry needs. It follows then that discovering and developing unique leadership styles is another major key to leadership effectiveness.

Andy Stanley, in his book *Next Generation Leader,* outlines five essentials for those who are future shapers:[3]

■ Competence: Leaders must channel their energies toward those arenas of leadership in which they are most likely to excel.

■ Courage: The leader of an enterprise isn't always the smartest or most creative person on the team. He isn't necessarily the first to identify an opportunity. The leader is the one who has the courage to initiate, to set things in motion, to move ahead.

- Clarity: Uncertain times require clear directives from those in leadership. Yet the temptation for young leaders is to allow uncertainty to leave them paralyzed. A next generation leader must learn to be clear even when he is not certain.

- Coaching: You may be good. You may even be better than everyone else. But without a coach you will never be as good as you could be.

- Character: You can lead without character, but you won't be a leader worth following. Character provides next generation leaders with the moral authority necessary to bring together the people and resources needed to further an enterprise.

John Maxwell is best known for his "21 Irrefutable Laws of Leadership." Let's review them, as he has them broken down for us in his book *The 21 Most Powerful Minutes in a Leader's Day*:[4]

- The law of THE LID: Leadership ability determines a person's level of effectiveness.

- The law of INFLUENCE: The true measure of leadership is influence: nothing more, nothing less.

- The law of PROCESS: Leadership develops daily, not in a day.

- The law of NAVIGATION: Anyone can steer the ship, but it takes a leader to chart the course.

- The law of E. F. HUTTON: When the real leader speaks, people listen.

- The law of SOLID GROUND: Trust is the foundation of leadership.

- The law of RESPECT: People naturally follow leaders stronger than themselves.

- The law of INTUITION: Leaders evaluate everything with a leadership bias.

- The law of MAGNETISM: Who you are is who you attract.

- The law of CONNECTION: Leaders touch a heart before they ask for a hand.

- The law of INNER CIRCLE: A leader's potential is determined by those closest to him.

- The law of EMPOWERMENT: Only secure leaders give power to others.

- The law of REPRODUCTION: It takes a leader to raise up a leader.

- The law of BUY-IN: People buy in to the leader, then the vision.

- The law of VICTORY: Leaders find a way for the team to win.

- The law of THE BIG MO: Momentum is the leader's best friend.

- The law of PRIORITIES: Leaders understand that activity is not necessarily accomplishment.

- The law of SACRIFICE: A leader must give up to go up.

- The law of TIMING: When to lead is as important as what to do and where to go.

- The law of EXPLOSIVE GROWTH: To add growth, lead followers—to multiply, lead leaders.

■ The law of LEGACY: A leader's lasting value is measured by succession.

In their book *Launching a Leadership Revolution*, Chris Brady and Orrin Woodward bring us into the concept of the "Five levels of Influence":[5]

1. Level one is LEARNING: The first of the levels of influence is becoming a student. Being hone-able and learning from others is a key to leadership success.

2. Level two is PERFORMANCE: The leader's accomplishments are mostly her own. Her influence extends only as far as her own ability to perform, and no further.

3. Level three is LEADING: Leadership is how a performer extends his or her ability through the efforts of others, to the betterment of everyone involved.

4. Level four is DEVELOPING LEADERS: At this level the leader increases his influence through the development of other leaders.

5. Level five is DEVELOPING LEADERS WHO DEVELOP LEADERS: This influence is seen on those rare occasions when a leader not only becomes very accomplished as a leader himself, and not only succeeds at developing other leaders, but manages to develop leaders who can then develop other leaders who continue the legacy onward.

I can't imagine where we would be today without the insights of men and women like these. They learned some of their lessons in the school of "hard knocks." Other lessons they learned as they went digging and looking for answers in desperate times. And then sometimes they were also blessed to receive a fresh revelation from heaven, via the Holy Spirit. However they received the understanding, we have all been blessed by them and others who cared enough to share their insights with us. Of course, being willing to learn from the wisdom and experience of others can at times be a challenge for us. Thankfully, God has a way of tugging on our pride and independence when we begin to resist opportunities to grow and learn. In fact, my prayer for you now is that the Holy Spirit will create a hunger and thirst for kingdom-sized leadership fruit that is so great in your ministry, you won't be able to take credit for it!

The information and training available from our peers and those who have gone before us is absolutely incredible. It doesn't make any difference what stream of the kingdom you and I relate to, there are books, CDs, DVDs, magazines, and seminars to help us to grow and be equipped for this unusual calling. Let's not forget the latest asset that is helping so many of us—coaches. These professional coaches will mentor and advise us from an offsite relationship. We *are* hungry for help. We *are* longing to be a success.

Since you are reading this book, you are probably not one who is satisfied with the way leadership is working for you. That's why I invited you to join me on this journey a few pages back. You and I long to have greater impact and bear good fruit along the way, but something just doesn't seem right. After all of the training and assistance we have received, it's as if there were still a piece missing from this puzzle—the piece that makes it complete and breathtaking. Without that missing piece, it just looks "nice" and your eyes always get drawn to that hole. Yes, there is still a piece missing here, a very valuable piece.

The time is the mid 1960s. I can hear and see her now. It's Peggy Lee on the black and white Motorola TV in my parent's living room on the *Dean Martin Show* singing "Is That All There Is?" For years my heart has echoed the words of that song. After doing my best and giving my life to this thing we call "church leadership," I knew that I was missing something. Many of our peers have let frustration get to them, and they are no longer standing before God's people. I refuse to accept that even after learning to develop the skills others have encouraged me to pursue, that this is all there is. If you can't find the words to express it, but you know what I mean, this book is for you.

Yes, there has been a piece missing, and no, this is not all there is.

Chapter 2
A PERSONAL REALITY CHECK

I T IS MAY 1980, and I've just unpacked my five boxes of books and "stuff." One of those unpacked items is a nameplate that now sits on the corner of my desk. My wife, Nina, presented it to me as a gift when I received my license to preach. There it sat in all its plastic woodgrain and brass glory: REV. MAX MYERS. "Reverend"—the weight of the title suddenly began to sink in. I was now the pastor of my first church. It was a small church that had split in half some months before our arrival. That now made "Peace Chapel" in Morris, Illinois, a "smaller" church. Let me tell you, there wasn't much peaceful about those years.

While preparing for vocational ministry through college and seminary, it all looks like it should be a "piece of cake." You are filled with the conviction that the events others experienced before you will never happen under your leadership. Ignorance is such bliss! It was at that moment of staring across the desk in that tiny office that the bliss came crashing down. I remember clearly thinking, "What in the world am I doing here?" Suddenly all of the confidence in my ability to be a good leader went right out the window.

To say that the years that followed were "interesting" would be an understatement. I'm having a hard time remembering which one of the many church growth seminars that I attended prepared me for not seeing—for three years—even one visitor walk through the doors of the church. Now I remember. None.

I also must have missed the seminary class the day they talked about what to do when the dear saint who is mad at you demands that all of the money she has ever given to the church be returned to her (along with all of the items she has purchased for the church). I must have been daydreaming on the day they talked about what to do when a board member shows up at your desk, hollering until he is red in the face, and slams down his church keys, never to be seen again. Oh yes, and then there was the day that the church parking lot caught on fire. If you ever see me, ask me about that story. It's a good one.

It was while pastoring Peace Chapel that I began to hunger for more leadership training. It was also at Peace Chapel that I learned the value of having a mentor. I owe my life ministry to one man, a board member, who would pull his Chevy pick-up into the parking lot every Monday morning to check on his pastor.

Gene Corlew was a successful local roofing contractor. He loved God, his family, and his pastor. A lump comes to my throat as I think about those conversations while leaning on the hood of his pick-up. I was frustrated, confused, and felt like a failure. All these years later, I can still hear his voice, "Brother Myers, you are doing the best anyone could do. What is happening is not your fault. Just hang in there. It will turn around."

Gene was right. After six years of ministry, we left behind a happy, growing, healthy, debt-free bunch of people. It was in this first season of church leadership that I began to question what it means to lead God's people, a question that would only get louder as years of ministry continued to pass.

My next season in the school of leadership would take us to Waupaca, Wisconsin. We wanted to build the kingdom, so we threw ourselves into the challenges before us. New young families began to fill up the chairs around those who had been in the church for years. Thousands of people would come through our doors each Christmas and Easter to hear and see our seasonal music/drama productions, with many giving their lives to Christ. Care groups, married couple's classes, and children's ministries had the church humming.

While everything looked really good to the naked eye, few knew about what was going on in the board meetings. I had blessed the process, which resulted in me having some men on the board who didn't agree with my vision and priorities. It proved to be a very valuable lesson and a very costly lesson for my family and me.

It was mid-January 1992 at the annual church business meeting. I had at this point been their pastor for six years, and it was time for a vote of the members as to whether or not I should remain their pastor for the next three years. Many of you know what that looks and feels like.

According to the church bylaws, I had to have two-thirds of the ballots cast in my favor in order to be retained. I had sensed in my spirit for the previous six months that something was up, but I couldn't find anyone near me who also sensed it. They said things like, "What are you concerned about? You have record growth, record Sunday school attendance, and record giving. Besides that, the people love you."

I was relieved of my ministry on that winter night by two votes.

My family and I were learning how painful local church leadership can be. Let me assure you, this kind of experience is *very* painful. I honor Chuck Gamm, a local businessman and board member who prayed for me and refused to let me walk that season alone.

At this point I began wrestling with what it means to provide God's people with leadership at an elevated level. Church leadership was forming in my mind as a system that was much more complicated and unpredictable than I had imagined or had been led to believe.

There was also something else beginning to gnaw on my spirit. Even though I understood as a pastor that I had stepped into an arena where my role, position, and authority had been predefined in previous generations, that model wasn't sitting right with me. I had given the church vision and mission. I had raised up and empowered small group leaders. I had put together outreaches that were impacting the community. I was visiting the elderly. I had facilitated yearly board retreats for accountability, relationship building, and goal setting. I had taken them through the process of preparing to break ground for badly needed expansion. I was showing up three mornings a week at 7 a.m. for small group prayer. I was integrating my life into the local community outside of the church. It didn't add up, so I proceeded to convince myself that I just had not learned the right leadership lessons yet. Any shortcomings or weaknesses in the church systems I dealt with were no doubt a reflection of my own personal shortcomings and weaknesses. At least, that offered some explanation for the train wreck.

Nina and I refused to let the pain of rejection keep us from doing what we had in our hearts to do—shepherd God's people into greener pastures. That determination led us to Riverside Assembly of God, in Hutchinson, Minnesota. We walked into that church still bleeding from our last experience, only to find that they had blood all over the church from problems that had escalated over the previous year.

We all wondered what would be the fruit of combining a beat-up pastor with a beat-up church. Over the next couple of years what we got was healing for our family and healing for the church. What a God! Together we experienced His life and presence in ways that I never imagined possible.

The church agreed at the front end of our relationship to

set me free to lead them wherever I felt we should go. They honored that promise, and those first seven years were a dream come true. Of course there were challenges, but we faced them together. That leadership togetherness allowed us to experience an outpouring of His presence for two years. The results? Thousands of people from all over the Midwest streamed through our doors. As was the case in Waupaca, thousands also came each Easter and Christmas to experience the powerful messages through drama and music.

On one hand, the years at Riverside were fourteen wonderful years of my life. On the other hand, there came a point where it became evident that I needed to step away. I longed to be free. I didn't know where my journey would take me, but my prayer life was being drawn to seek some God revelation on kingdom leadership. It was in this leadership season that I began to ask God questions about why churches function as they do. Over the following two years, He began to answer those questions, and to set me free.

All of us who are in this leadership journey have stories that are unique to our environments. The thumbnail description of my personal experiences has been shared with you for the purpose of giving you an understanding of where I have been. If you can capture where I have been, it will be easier for you to capture where I am going, and what motivated me to go there.

Step back with me for a moment, and let's look at the broader landscape of what church leadership looks like in this generation. I'm not considering what our specific leadership fruit looks like in our churches and ministries. I'm talking about looking at the personal condition of leaders themselves. What do men and women look like when they aren't putting their best foot forward as church and ministry leaders?

Dropouts

The probability that someone beginning vocational pastoral ministry as a young person will reach retirement age as a pastor is alarmingly low. The cost of leadership becomes higher than we ever expected to pay. Let's face it. Leading God's people is wonderful, but the challenges that go with it are sometimes more than we bargained for. Of course there are a wide variety of reasons as to why pastors choose to step out of leadership. There is, though, one basic common denominator: something else became more attractive than pastoral ministry.

I am presently training a group of men and women to become pastors and leaders. At times I find myself apologizing to these students. No matter what the topic of the day is, I find myself spending time on *what to watch out for*. At times I have had to do some prayerful soul-searching about my motives. I've also had the experience of receiving training from leaders who have had a chip on their shoulder, and I want to be certain not to be one of those. Really, the reason I spend time talking with my students about the challenges of ministry leadership, is because I don't want them to drop out. I want them to understand the challenges before them and sign on to see their calling through to the end.

For a growing number of people, the answer to the stress, pressure, and disappointment is to step out of leadership and try the grass on the other side of the fence. For many of you, it looks lush and green over there right now. Hold on! Just stay with me and walk with me through this journey.

Broken Homes

There are two kinds of broken homes in ministry. One type has been broken in public viewing for all to see. The other type is broken, but those outside the home have been prevented from seeing what is really going on. For the most part, pastoral homes are a reflection of the culture they dwell with. Pastors' homes have to face the same challenges everyone else does. Finances, communication, in-laws, health issues, parenting, conflict, disagreement, accidents, unexpected disaster, schedules, unmet expectations, and lack of intimacy are common in the parsonage. Now add to that being on call 24/7, along with a list of expectations from those you serve that you can never live up to. The result in many pastors' homes is a breakdown in relationships. Sometimes it is the children who fail to comply with the expectations of the home and begin to rebel. Other times it can be between the pastor and spouse. These seasons of family breakdown can be lived out publicly, or encapsulated out of public view. Both scenarios are painful and genuinely have an impact on the pastor's ability to lead the flock. The relational pain in many pastors' homes is enormous, with many marriages staying together purely for the purpose of keeping their credentials and employment.

Immorality

Some pastors choose to ease the pain and stress of leadership through relationships outside of marriage. Of course, this choice leads to an increase of pain and stress to all who love and respect them. I'm not sure how pollsters are able to get an honest answer from pastors on this question when they ask about extramarital affairs. The percentage of those who respond with the affirmative is so high, I shudder to think of what it would be if they all told the truth.

So what's going on here? Why so much unfaithfulness in the pastor's home? Consider this. How have we been trained to think as leaders? We are trained to have a vision for what we want, then develop a plan to get it. What I would like to point out is that the training that's meant to enable church growth, works equally as well for pastors who want something they think they can't get at home, even if they shouldn't have it. Of course, there are more dynamics in play than just this one. Whatever the circumstances are, one thing is evident. This generation of church leaders has a fading revelation of the need for personal responsibility and holiness.

Addictions

This arena of attempted leadership stress release has gone "through the roof." Illegal and prescription drug use is growing. Alcoholism in ministry homes is abundant. Pornography in printed form, through videos and on the Internet is rolling through pastors' homes and offices like a freight train. On several occasions, I have had the responsibility of showing up at the door of a pastor's home (as a representative of my denomination) and asking the pastor to turn over his personal computer to me. This unfortunate event unfolds because someone close to the pastor has turned in evidence of their potential pornography addiction. The computer is turned over to a computer business that looks for evidence of porn site visits on their hard drive. I've never been involved in a case where the evidence wasn't there. I've also never been involved in a case where the pastor confessed when first approached. They all denied it until the hard drive report showed otherwise. What an interesting observation.

Whether it be alcohol, drugs, gambling, or pornography, the people that we are training up to be leaders are struggling with their ability to be free from life-controlling behaviors.

Kingdom Empire Building

The primary standard set for church leaders is big ministry, big budget, big car, big smile, and big salary. After all, in our culture what could be a better measure for success? The process that many pastors establish is to build a kingdom with only one star of the show—me. Now that's an interesting phenomena for people called to be servants. Primarily due to the illegal and immoral behavior of some in our ranks, our culture no longer offers unquestioning respect to pastors. One of the ways that some pastors have chosen to walk in order to attempt to gain respect is by creating a personal "wow" factor. The use of electronic media and technology has been very helpful at creating an aura of greatness by selling to the public a perception of our greatness.

Beat Up and Stressed Out

Pastors do the best they can, but the best isn't normally good enough—not for the pastors, their spouses, or the people they serve. Congregations are demanding that we meet all of their needs, and leadership teams are waiting for pastors to put together the perfect strategy that will answer all those needs. On top of it all, God must surely be disappointed in us, because we seem unable to meet the expectations that we are convinced He has of us. We're eating more food. Not sleeping. Unhappy.

Maybe you have noticed that I didn't use any "hard data" as we looked over the pastoral leadership landscape. There is a reason for that. For you leaders, the latest poll numbers and survey results are pointless. You are living it. You know what is happening in your life and the lives of our peers. For some of us, the leadership life really isn't too bad. We have learned to adapt and manage along the way to survive. For others, it's not just bad. It's ugly.

It's time for some simple reflection. The God of the universe put His hand on you and set you aside to lead His flock, and build His kingdom. Was "ugly" what He had in mind when He called you? Was He thinking, "I hope that they survive this"? I don't think so.

Something is very wrong with this picture.

Chapter 3
I'M EQUIPPED, YET
SOMETHING'S MISSING

Y OU CAN ACCUMULATE a lot of stuff in an office over fourteen years—stuff you "might" need some day. One of the advantages of growing older in the ministry is that when you box up your office to move to another location, you now know what you will use in the future and what you won't. I threw out or gave away at least half of my office library on one particular day. Why drag it along with you if you'll never use it again?

While on my knees clearing out the base cabinet of the bookcase, I opened the doors to my huge stacks of *Leadership* magazines. I'm pretty sure that I had saved every issue from the publication's inception. When it would arrive in the mail, I would immediately hunt for the most important thing first—the cartoons. Once I had chuckled over them and read a few to my wife, I would go back to the beginning and start reading the articles. Those volumes in my bookcase contained insightful information about everything that pastors could possibly encounter or need to know. *Leadership* and other fine publications are doing all that they can to equip leaders for the opportunities and challenges ahead. Periodicals are not our only source for leadership training, as we are blessed with an abundance of other leadership growth and equipping resources. Let's consider them for a moment.

Books

As I mentioned in chapter one, there are an amazing number of books written for church leaders. You probably have a number in your possession. Chances are that you didn't even need to buy most of them. Some came from dear friends or saints who knew it would be a "blessing." Of course, what our self-talk would sometimes say is, "They think I need some more help." That's not such a bad thing is it? The fact that you are reading this book already says something about how you view what is happening in your leadership life.

Have you ever noticed how patient a book is while it sits on your desk, bookcase, or nightstand? I received a book from a family member a number of years ago that was recommended by their pastor at the church they attended. It sat in my bookcase for about eight years. One day Nina and I were preparing for a long international fight, and I began looking over my collection of books for something and it caught my attention. I pulled out that long-neglected book and brought it with me on the journey. Little did I know that I was about to go on two journeys at the same time. The message between those two covers completely transformed how I viewed one specific area of ministry and theology. It brought answers to questions I was asking and clarity to issues that I had been uncomfortable with. So, what's my point? If I would have read that book when I received it, its message would not have resonated with my spirit, and I would not have been impacted by it. Isn't the gentle nudging ministry of the Holy Spirit amazing? That book sat patiently on my shelf, waiting for me to get ready for its message.

For generations past and generations to come, books will be one of God's powerful instruments for revelation of His heart and will for His people. We are all stronger, wiser, and healthier as a result of what we have read.

Seminars

If you have been in ministry for any length of time at all, you have probably traveled somewhere to take in a training, equipping seminar. At these events we are able to "get away" for a few days and sit under some of the nation's most influential leaders. We fill up the pages of our notebooks with words of wisdom and creative ideas that we all wish we would have thought of first. Actually, there is an interesting dynamic that takes place as the ink is flying onto the pages across the room. What is systematically happening is that we are all processing the potential for our own personal success with what we are hearing about. If you can risk being honest with me, you will admit that by and large, we end up rejecting most of what we hear. Some of that rejection is immediate and occurs spontaneously as we hear of the speaker's experiences and insights. Our filters rationalize that "It would never work in my church. They don't have a budget restriction like mine. They don't have a board like mine. They don't have a community like mine." You get the picture.

Other rejections of what we are taught come a little later. This is the "It sounded good at the time" syndrome. The buy-in with the conclusion that what I first embraced isn't for me, can set in anywhere from the next meal conversation to weeks down the road. In this scenario our conclusion is normally not based on how we view the restrictions of our environment, as much as it is how we view our personal ability to be able to incorporate what we have just learned.

Training seminars provided by ministries, networks, and denominations definitely have their limitations, yet they also serve church leadership in an effective way. In spite of what I previously described, we do catch some of what comes our way. We also benefit from the opportunity to get away from our daily environment, which allows us the opportunity to gain perspective about a number of ministry issues that we just couldn't see while home. Nina and I always go deeper in our communication concerning both personal and ministry issues when we are away from home. Seminars serve as one of our primary methods of church leadership development.

Downloads and Online Courses

Only time will reveal the real fruit of our use of technology. As electronic communication increasingly replaces face-to-face, real time relationships, we in church have learned to adapt to the life of electronic relationships. We can now listen to or watch leadership training whenever we want. It's as simple as paying a few dollars, then downloading the training into our electronic devices. Wherever we are, whenever we want, someone is there to train us. Ongoing training is also available to us by enrolling in online leadership courses. We can receive instruction at our desktops, on our laptops, or in our handheld device whenever we want. The world of downloads and online training has really opened up a whole new level of available leadership instruction. There are several factors that make it appealing.

The first thing that electronic training has going for it is that it is equally available to everyone. All you need is to be able to get online, and have a charge card to pay for it. The computer doesn't care about your denomination, age, race, or education. It doesn't care about whether you are a heathen or a saint. Everyone can equally search and find the training of their choice, even if their church or denomination would never endorse it.

The second thing that electronic training has going for it is that it puts the leader in charge of the schedule in which it will be listened to or watched. Only have time to take in thirty minutes worth? Fine. Just pick up where you left off when you have time to devote to it again. You don't need to ask your governing board for time off to travel somewhere for several days of training. You can get it right in your office or in the comfort of your home.

The third thing that electronic training has going for it is that it is very cost effective. To get similar training in person would normally involve a combination of the following:

- Seminar/class registration costs
- Gasoline, airfare, car rental, airport parking
- Meals
- Lodging

Obviously, whatever the charge may be for purchasing electronic leadership training, it pales in comparison to the costs of onsite training.

Coaches

One of the latest leadership tools to be developed is the concept of a personal coach or mentor. Unlike periodicals, books, seminars, and electronic media, a coach enters into a personal interactive relationship with the pastor. A leadership coach will initially invest a considerable amount of time in the following:

- Developing an understanding of the pastor's ministry environment

- Evaluating the pastor's ministry gifts and weaknesses

- Determining what the pastor's patterns of leadership have been

- Assessing and clarifying the leader's vision for his or her ministry

The frequency of contact between the coach and leader is normally predetermined when the contractual relationship is agreed upon upfront. Contact can range from weekly to monthly, and normally occurs by phone. Payment for the service of a coach is normally based upon the length of the contract and the frequency of the contact between them.

Generally, the role of a coach is not that of a person who tells the pastor what to do in a given situation. The overall goal of a coach is to help the leader develop the skills to be able to make his or her own healthy and productive decisions. Most coaches strive to help pastors identify their options, followed by helping the pastor through the process of choosing the best option. Having an individual who is able to make real-time assessments through a pastor's leadership journey is a considerable strength for this training model.

Without a doubt, this is the best-trained, best-equipped generation of leaders up to date. If you are willing to take advantage of it, there is training and support at every turn. At this point we need to ask one question of these resources. The question is: What are the models and methods that church leaders are being trained to walk in?

Here are my observations in response to that question.

Identify Goals

We are trained to clarify what the goals are for our ministry. What do we want to create? What do we want to accomplish? Where do we want the local church to go? What do we want to eliminate or avoid? To be honest, much of our prayer life and administrative energy is invested into this arena of identifying our goals. The reason, of course, is simple. If we want to get somewhere, we first have to determine where it is that we want to go.

A term that is often used as synonymous with goal-setting is the biblical concept of having a "vision." A vision is defined as the ability to anticipate and make provision for future events. Whichever terminology you use—having a goal for your ministry, or having a vision for your ministry—the end result is similar. We are simply painting a mental image of how we want things to look in the future under our leadership.

Build Systems

Most leadership training is geared toward the process of building systems that will get us to our goals. The definition of a system is "the orderly combination or arrangements of parts into a whole, according to some rational principle." So system-building then is a process that we go through where we figure out what will need to be done on a step-by-step basis in order to achieve our goals.

To meet our goals, we need to be able to plan for the journey that will get us there. To engage our culture, we develop systems and strategies that we hope will give us a reasonable level of success. To disciple our flock, we develop systems that will move them from point A to point B. You see, almost everything we do is connected to a system, process, and strategy. When we get our arms around that reality, it then becomes very reasonable as to why we need the training and coaching in this area on an ongoing basis. When the success of our goals depends on the quality and accuracy of our systems, then learning how to build good systems is crucial.

Learn from Successful Models

Many of the "how to" models that we are learning about are models that did not originate from the church, but from the corporate business community. A number of books in my library on team-building, reaching goals, and developing a quality product were not written for the church. They were written for the corporate environment, discovered by Christian leaders, and recommended to us as a good read with principles that can be applied to our church situations. In the corporate world, success is not an option. Why? Because if your business strategy is not successful, you will not be profitable. If your business isn't profitable, jobs are lost and lives are adversely affected. Since success is not an option, they have learned methods that will help ensure success. You and I would like to raise our ability to be successful, so we gather all we can from the leaders of the business sector of our culture. In reality, much of what we have taught through generations of church leadership are methods we've picked up from our culture.

Measurable Goals

We are trained to measure things. How close are we to this goal? How far away are we from that goal? If we can measure and get our bearings, we can plan a strategy from that point forward. What we are learning about measurable goals is this: If I am meeting my goals, I am a success. If I have not meeting my goals, I have failed. Don't you just hate the sound of that word? Like it or not, that is our reality, so let's keep looking at how failure affects us.

If we are failing to meet our goals, our training tells us that it will primarily be because of one of these three reasons:

Our system was faulty.

The process we put together to get us to the goal had some problems in its execution that sidetracked it, and caused it to fall short.

Our team was incapable of carrying out the system we developed.

Somebody "dropped the ball" along the journey. In order to reach our goals, in most cases our process for getting there will involve the assistance or cooperation of others. When the team that we have assembled includes people that do not or are not capable of carrying through the portion of the system that they were responsible for, the success of the goal is greatly jeopardized.

We didn't work hard enough.

If we would have conducted more meetings, made more phone calls, sent out more mail, or knocked on a few more doors, our goals would have been met, and we would have been successful. Somewhere along the line, our attention became diverted to other pressing issues, and we just weren't able to achieve the goal.

Summary

In reality, there has never been a generation before us that has been better equipped to lead than our generation. We have invested large sums of money and countless hours into becoming the best leaders we can be. Many of us have been developing our leadership skills, and thankfully they have gotten us further than we would have without the training.

Let's put leadership training into bodybuilding terms; in order for us to build up our strength we put our body through a number of disciplines. We lift weights and put our muscles through intense pressure, which increases our muscle mass. We run so that our cardio-vascular system is strengthened. We modify our diet, eating those foods that will assist us with the level of nutrition that our bodies need. After following this regimen over time, we should be able to experience tangible fruit from our effort. Two of those results will be that we can now lift more weight and run further than we could before we started to work out.

The same principle is true for us as we develop our leadership skills. After years of leadership training and working it into our ministry lives, we can achieve more and do it better than we would have without the training. We have developed leadership "muscle." Of course, the results vary for each one of us just like it does in bodybuilding. It has a lot to do with what we start out with. Just as each individual has a limit to his or her potential in bodybuilding, the same principle holds true with our leadership development. How far I can go has a lot to do with what I bring to work with. On the other hand, how far I go has a lot to do with how hard I work at learning and applying myself to the systems, structures, and processes for ministry success.

It is at this place of realization that I must again point to a level of discomfort that I have with this whole package that we have learned to simply call "leadership development." We will build on it in the chapters to come, but let me give you a glimpse into the tension I see, feel, and experience at this juncture.

Basically what I have just described for you in this chapter is a process of church leadership development that has *everything* to do with *our* abilities. How *I* can build this system. How *I* can carry out the process. How *I* can achieve my goals.

Of course, we can find Bible personalities and scriptural illustrations to validate almost all of our techniques. Even so, why does the end conclusion of our present leadership training affirm that ministry leadership is all about *me*? Who decided along the way that leading God's people into their destiny and enlarging the kingdom was dependent on my skill development? You might be thinking, "So what's the big deal? Sure it is about my abilities." This is of concern to me for two reasons.

First, here is what Scripture says about the building the church:

> Unless the LORD builds the house, they labor in vain who build it.
>
> —PSALM 127:1

I also say to you that you are Peter, and upon this rock
I will build My church; and the gates of Hades will not
overpower it.

—MATTHEW 16:18

What I clearly see here is that God feels He is quite capable
of building His church. What a novel concept.

My second concern is this: if leading God's people and
moving them into measurable success is primarily based on
learning and applying systems and processes, then an unbe-
liever could do it. Yes, you read it right. A person living outside
of a right relationship with God and His Word could build a
"successful" church simply by applying learned leadership and
systems principles. *Hmmmm.* Just now, some of you thought of
someone that you know of like that. Call it what you want to.
Color it any way you choose. In the end, the truth is that something is amiss with our leadership model.

For years as a pastor, I reached out for a blurry image of
leadership that I knew had to exist—a leadership that wasn't all
about me. When I would reach out to it, it would slip away. My
spirit called out for it, even though I didn't have a clear understanding of what it was. You know what I'm talking about. It is
in your spirit as well.

Come along. The journey is about to get interesting.

Chapter 4
THE ROUTE THAT WAS CHOSEN

W E ALL HAVE things we like to do when we're not on the job, and for me it's doing something that will get me dirty. I was raised on a working farm in Illinois and I love to just "take on projects." One of my motivations for taking on all kinds of projects has been the fact that I am a minister. I couldn't afford to pay for much of what I often needed done, so I had to figure out how to do it myself.

Some years ago, Nina and I built a beautiful home on a trout stream in central Wisconsin. To save money, I decided to do a lot of the work myself. With some much-needed instruction from contractors in my church, I did my own plumbing and wiring and also stained, varnished, and installed all of the trim. If any of you have thought about trimming your own home, I have one word of advice: don't! I was never able to fully enjoy any room in that house over the years we lived in it. When I sat down in a room, my eyes always fell on the cut that didn't match up just right.

While cutting a board on my table saw one afternoon, my left hand got too close to the blade and I removed a good portion of the inside of that thumb. In time the skin grew back, but for years the nerve endings in that area were extremely sensitive to touch. During the healing process I began to develop new patterns of holding things in my left hand. I even developed a different way of squeezing toothpaste out of the tube in order to protect the affected thumb area from contact. That table saw accident happened about twenty years ago, and I now have normal skin sensitivity on the damaged area. But, guess what? I *still* hold the toothpaste tube the way I did when it was hurt. I still rotate the tube into a position that protects my thumb without thinking, each time I pick it up.

Could this be an example of how our church leadership styles have developed? Could it be that years and generations ago something happened at a "leadership moment" that changed the course for that particular situation, yet years and generations later we find that we are still "protecting that area"? Could it be that some of what we naturally do and teach as church leadership was not originally God's plan, but we have grown accustomed to the alternative along the way? I believe so.

Historically, we have done a good job of going to the Word to find chapters and verses that fit our philosophical leadership approach. On this journey, we are going to look at the progression and development of leadership, as it is played out for us from the beginning in Scripture.

Early Old Testament Progression of Leadership

Genesis 1:28 states:

> God blessed them; and God said to them, "Be fruitful and multiply, and fill the earth, and subdue it; and rule over the fish of the sea and over the birds of the sky and over every living thing that moves on the earth."

In this simple encounter, we have God's first recorded communication with Adam, the first human.

Note that these first recorded words aren't, "Hello, I'm God and I have been looking forward to this special moment." God doesn't say, "You have been made in my image and I perfectly love you." God's first recorded words to Adam were words of instruction. *Be fruitful. Multiply yourself over the earth. Bring the rest of creation under your authority* (Gen. 1:22). By giving Adam instructions in their first encounter, God is setting up an important foundation for the rest of their relationship. He is communicating to Adam, "I am giving you responsibility, purpose, and freedom. Just remember this: you are accountable to Me."

In chapters 6 and 7 of Genesis, God gave Noah His rationale for destroying creation.

> Then the LORD said to Noah, "Enter the ark, you and all your household, for you alone I have seen to be righteous before Me in this time."
>
> —GENESIS 7:1

Here we have another leadership first. This is the first time the Bible records that God gave an individual instructions directly requiring him to incorporate others. Prior to this, all recorded God encounters dealt with God's personal direction and expectations of the individual. Now with Noah, He begins to expand Noah's responsibility to the leadership of others. A pattern begins to develop.

> Now the LORD said to Abram, "Go forth from your country, And from your relatives, And from your father's house, To the land which I will show you: And I will make you a great nation, And I will bless you, And make your name great; And so you shall be a blessing."
>
> —GENESIS 12:1–2

Here, the Lord spoke to Abram with directions and promises concerning what he was to do, and how he was to lead his family. This pattern continued throughout his life. It was a simple pattern. First, God spoke to Abram in a manner that he could understand. Second, God expected Abram to take that instruction and lead others with it (Gen. 12:7, 13:14–17, 15:1, 16:11–12, 17:1–21, 18:17–21, 21:12–13, 22:1–17). Next, the Lord appeared to Isaac in Genesis 26:2–4 with personal leadership instructions.

> The LORD appeared to him and said, "Do not go down to Egypt; stay in the land of which I shall tell you. Sojourn in this land and I will be with you and bless you, for to you and to your descendants I will give all these lands, and I will establish the oath which I swore to your father Abraham. I will multiply your descendants as the stars of heaven, and will give your descendants all these lands; and by your descendants all the nations of the earth shall be blessed."
>
> —GENESIS 26:2–4

In Genesis 28:13–15, the Lord appeared to Jacob with a promise and instruction concerning His plans through Jacob. As with those before him, this pattern was repeated (Gen. 31:3, 31:12–13, 35:1, 35:9–12). The process continued with Joseph and then moved to a whole new level with Moses. From the burning bush encounter to the end of his lifetime, God consistently gave Moses directions as to how and where He wanted Moses to move His people. Sometimes in Scripture we are given a location for these encounters such as Mt. Sinai with the giving of the law, or in the Tent of Meeting. Other times we aren't given a location, just a record of the conversation.

What I want us to see is that when we evaluate what is happening sequentially in Scripture, we see that from Adam on, God is establishing a pattern of how He wants His people led. It is very simple. It is very plain. It is very clear. God wants to lead and guide His people, personally, through individuals of His choice. We have a term for that kind of a leadership relationship: it's called a *theocracy*. Most of us are familiar with the term. *Theocracy* means "God-guided." As we see it demonstrated in the Old Testament texts, theocracy is *God influencing His people, through those that He chooses to use.*

First Samuel 7 offers a perfect example of how it was all meant to work.

> Then the sons of Israel said to Samuel, "Do not cease to cry to the LORD our God for us, that He may save us from the hand of the Philistines." Samuel took a suckling lamb and offered it for a whole burnt offering to the LORD; and Samuel cried to the LORD for Israel and the LORD answered him. Now Samuel was offering up the burnt offering, and the Philistines drew near to battle against Israel. But the LORD thundered with a great thunder on that day against the Philistines and confused them, so that they were routed before Israel. The men of Israel went out of Mizpah and pursued the Philistines, and struck them down as far as below Beth-car.
>
> —1 SAMUEL 7:8–11

What do we see happening here? First, as I mentioned before, we see God speaking through the person of His choice. Second, when threats or challenges came to God's people, the leader looked to God for divine assistance. There was a core understanding that God had the ability to work out the details of their impossible situations. They knew God to have all the power that they would need to succeed. The third thing we see illustrated in 1 Samuel 7 is that divine intervention does arrive for God's people. It is a testimony to His people, and unbelieving nations alike, of His power, justice, and faithfulness. This is what makes God's original plan of theocracy so unique. It is not only in our best interest, it is also in His best interest as well.

The plan wasn't just about God getting His way through people who would cooperate with Him. It was about God intervening on behalf of His people, in *supernatural* ways—Noah's ark, parting the Red Sea, manna, water from a rock, Jericho, fiery furnace, lion's den, Elijah vs. prophets of Baal, and so on. God loved to intervene in our natural world with supernatural power, and I have a hunch that He still feels that way.

Theocracy was His first plan. It was a good plan. Why? It was a good plan because it was *His* plan. (Now that's a point we can't argue with!) Theocracy was a good plan because it always depended upon *Him*, not on education or training, and not on a person's ability to come up with successful strategies and formulas. The outcome of theocracy was always dependent upon three things:

1. God's direction
2. Man's willingness to cooperate with that direction
3. God's response and activity

The Shift

Theocracy *was* a great plan. Yet, during the prophet Samuel's generation, God's people were in full-blown rebellion against His plans for their welfare. It was with this generation that things began to shift. It was with this generation that a new foundation was laid, the foundation that we are still building on today. Let's follow the sequence of events recorded in 1 Samuel 8:1–3. In these verses we find that Samuel appointed his sons as judges over all of Israel. According to v. 3, his sons were not concerned with the ways of God. They used their power and authority for their own gain, took bribes, and chose not to judge fairly. Things were not well in Israel.

As a result of their national condition, the elders presented Samuel a revolutionary plan that is recorded in the latter portion of verse 5.

…and they said to him, "Behold, you have grown old, and your sons do not walk in your ways. Now appoint a king for us to judge us like all the nations."

—1 SAMUEL 8:5

Samuel understood what the implications were of such a leadership shift, so he took their request to God and God responded.

The LORD said to Samuel, "Listen to the voice of the people in regard to all that they say to you, for they have not rejected you, but they have rejected Me from being king over them. Like all the deeds which they have done since the day that I brought them up from Egypt even to this day—in that they have forsaken Me and served other gods—so they are doing to you also."

—1 SAMUEL 8:7–8

It was a sad day for the kingdom. God's incredible, powerful, perfect plan of theocracy was being rejected. God told Samuel to give them what they want, but to warn them of the consequences. What an eloquent job Samuel did in verses 11–18 as he outlined what life would be like under human leadership instead of God's leadership.

He said, "This will be the procedure of the king who will reign over you: he will take your sons and place them for himself in chariots and among his horsemen, and they will run before his chariots. He will appoint for himself commanders of thousands and of fifties, and some to do his plowing and to reap his harvest and to make his weapons of war and equipment for his chariots. He will also take your daughters for perfumers and cooks and bakers. He will take the best of your fields and your vineyards and your olive groves and give them to his servants. He will take a tenth of your seed and of your vineyards and give to his officers and to his servants. He will also take your male servants and your female servants and your best young men and your donkeys and use them for his work. He will take a tenth of your flocks, and you yourselves will become his servants. Then you will cry out in that day because of your king whom you have chosen for yourselves, but the LORD will not answer you in that day."

—1 SAMUEL 8:11–18

One truth is very evident here. Rejecting God's rule and choosing another model has a very high price. Samuel could not have warned them *or us* any more clearly. Here is the elder's response to Samuel:

Nevertheless, the people refused to listen to the voice of Samuel, and they said, "No, but there shall be a king over us, that we also may be like all the nations, that our king may judge us and go out before us and fight our battles."

—1 SAMUEL 8:19–20

I know that you already understand how important foundations are. The stability, security, and alignment of everything built on top of a foundation is subject to the condition of the foundation. In this event between God, Samuel, and the Elders, a new foundation was laid for the way God's people would be lead. What is that foundation made of? Look at it yourself:

"For they have not rejected you, but they have rejected Me from being king over them."

—1 SAMUEL 8:7

Rejection. Our present leadership model has been built on the rejection of God as King. Oh, my!

One phrase from the people's response also rings so loud, it is almost deafening: "That we also may be like all the nations." Except for the "Jesus season" and early apostolic period, the declaration of these elders has been the pattern we have followed for thousands of years. From Samuel's anointing of Saul as the first king, through today, we have had generation after generation born as the fruit of their call "that we may also be like all the nations."

It would be comfortable to point a finger at our secular culture and decry their choices. It might bring me some satisfaction if I could blame our moral and political environment for what has been happening in the church. The truth of the matter is that thousands of years ago, a choice was made for us by our spiritual forefathers. They chose that His people would no longer be ruled by Him, but by *self*. Self says, "We can do it better than He can. We can build better structure. We can build better systems. We can build better programs. We can lead people better."

What kind of fruit has this "better way than theocracy" given us in the church? Today's church looks just like all the nations. Let the weight of what we have just uncovered settle into your spirit. This is serious stuff.

Our forefathers sliced off the side of their thumb. The pain from their wound caused them to form new leadership styles, systems, and motives. Out of habit we are still protecting that old pain by doing things like we have for generations, even though we are fully capable of functioning like we were originally created to function.

- It's time for us to end self-rule.

- It's time to relook at God's original design for how His kingdom is to be led.

- It's time for a new style of leadership.

- It's time for a new type of leader.

- It's time for supernatural leadership.

PART II:
PAINTING A NEW LANDSCAPE

Chapter 5
PUTTING INTO PLACE THE BACKGROUND COLORS

I F I WERE to personally ask each of you to describe your mental image of Jesus' appearance, I am quite certain that the pool of responses would identify several recurring themes. Most of you would include:

- Brown, wavy, collar- to shoulder-length hair
- Brown, trimmed beard
- Deep-set eyes
- Strong jawbone features
- Slight, thin build

Obviously, we have no way of confirming His actual appearance. In fact, scholars have weighed in on the topic to share with us that some of the features listed above probably do not reflect reality. But who needs reality? My simple request that you think about what Jesus looked like brought up a picture in your mind.

Where did that picture come from? It came from the picture of Jesus hanging in your Sunday school classroom when you were a child. It came from the pictures in your Bible. It came from the stained-glass window in your church. From time to time on your journey you have seen various artists' impressions of what Jesus looked like. Because you have looked at those images over the years, they now form the only image that you can see with your imagination.

In essence, the same thing has been true with our picture of church leadership. One common picture of what church leadership looks like has been painted by those who have gone before us, generation after generation. There have been some slight variations in this picture, just like there have been slight variations in the artists' depictions of Jesus. Yet, like the image we all have of Jesus, the central components of church leadership are the same across the board.

It's time for a new picture. It will no longer work for us to keep using the same picture of leadership that has been passed to us. That picture has as its foundation the development of natural abilities, along with pursuit of a model that has been established by secular culture. That picture was founded on the rejection of God as the ultimate authority over His church. In this chapter we will begin to put into place the background colors that will serve as a new foundation for details to be added in later chapters. For the rest of our new picture to make sense, there are a number of things that we need to look at together. Let's get underway with a fresh new blank canvas.

What we are looking to create is not just a *process* for developing great leaders. That is what has been done for generations. When the decision was made to move from theocracy to human-rule, it became imperative that personal skills be developed to raise the potential for a successful outcome. Look where it has gotten us. If human-rule leadership isn't what we are looking for, then what kind of leadership do we want to establish?

Simply put, this new picture is about *supernatural leadership*. At its core, the "supernatural" realm functions outside of the limitations of the natural realm. The natural realm operates within boundaries that we can manipulate with human influences such as sight, speech, sound, touch, intelligence, strategizing, etc. "Supernatural" is not confined by the natural. Not only is it not confined by natural limitations, but the supernatural realm invades the natural realm and shifts its course. Why is it not confined? Because its source is the awesome mind, heart, and power of an incredible God. Jesus said that all things are possible with God. The natural cannot confine Him. Now that's supernatural!

Though there are many facets of supernatural leadership that are intriguing, one facet always captivates me. Since the source of the supernatural is our living God, then supernatural leadership by its nature also lives and breathes. Yes, it consists of tried and tested principles passed to us from generation to generation. But it also consists of inspired revelation direct from the heart of God. Supernatural leadership is a leadership relationship that is alive! Supernatural leadership is a leadership that is not confined to all of the constraints that we have been taught to deal with.

For years many of you, like me, have led God's people using the techniques and systems of development grounded in a heritage of what I call "natural leadership." We keep watching, hoping, and by all means praying that we would be one of those who see some significant results. By and large, most of us have been significantly disappointed. Why? We keep using *natural* leadership, and we keep looking for *supernatural* results. That is just not going to work. We are going to receive fruit in the form of the same type of seed that we sow. If you and I want to begin to see supernatural results in our ministry, we are going to need to begin walking in supernatural leadership

Five Basic Premises

1. Unlike natural leadership, supernatural leadership is at its core "simple" leadership.

Supernatural leadership is not based on a maze of processes, but instead on the simplicity of relationship. Natural leadership demands of us that we implement structures and systems, which in the end means that we have to create, maintain, and manage a lot of "hoops." There is absolutely nothing simple about how we do natural leadership. Supernatural leadership, on the other hand, focuses its energy into pursuing a relationship with the Father, then simply activating His direction. We will look at the development of this relationship in the chapters to come.

2. Jesus' life and ministry is our life and ministry model.

Many of us have bought into the frame of reference that Jesus as Messiah had the advantage of resources that are unavailable to us. Some want to believe that, because if it were true we would have an excuse for not measuring up to His leadership walk. Just take a moment to think about it with me. If Jesus lived out His ministry as God, with power and abilities not available to me, then what was that all about? Should we package the Gospels like a carnival side show? "Come one, come all to the great Jesus show. Step right up!" Absolutely not! Instead, He demonstrated a life to us that He promised we could live.

> Truly, truly, I say to you, he who believes in Me, the works that I do, he will do also; and greater works than these he will do; because I go to the Father.
>
> —John 14:12

> Therefore Jesus answered and was saying to them, "Truly, truly, I say to you, the Son can do nothing of Himself, unless it is something He sees the Father doing; for whatever the Father does, these things the Son also does in like manner."
>
> —John 5:19

> I can do nothing on My own initiative. As I hear, I judge; and My judgment is just, because I do not seek My own will, but the will of Him who sent Me.
>
> —John 5:30

Fortunately, the truth is that Jesus functioned with the personal and spiritual resources that are available to us. When we watch Jesus deal with issues that relate to leading people into the kingdom, we are watching Him unfold for us the Father's intent. Jesus was not an independent renegade. He walked out supernatural leadership in fascinating ways. Isn't that what your heart longs for? A leadership journey that is fascinating?

3. God likes His original plans, and wants to restore what we have messed up to its original state.

What God creates is always good. *Really* good! Scripture demonstrates that He wants to bring creation back to its original position in the story of the prodigal son. The son who leaves and messes up the Father's original plan is placed back into the position that he was in prior to his rebellion. In 1 Thessalonians 5:14–17, we read of the believers' graves opening and bodies being raised up to join their souls in heaven. Man messed up God's original plan for body, soul, and spirit to live together eternally in the Garden of Eden. In the end, He will make sure that it happens just like He had planned by bringing body, soul, and spirit together. God likes His original plans and desires to restore them. In like manner, God liked His plan to lead His people, through people who will get their direction from Him. In this generation He is looking for men and women like you who will impact the nations through supernatural theocratic leadership.

4. God wants to be very actively involved in the activities that surround His kingdom.

Contrary to popular songs of our culture like Bette Midler's "From a Distance," God is not watching us from a distance. The only distance that we have created between God and us is the distance between our ears.

> For the Father loves the Son, and shows Him all things that He Himself is doing; and the Father will show Him greater works than these, so that you will marvel.
>
> —JOHN 5:20

Let's think about it this way. Jesus says that the Father is busy doing things. Jesus says that He only does what He sees the Father doing. Jesus was actively involved with lives and His environment on a daily basis. That must mean that the Father is active and wants to be active through us. Such a deal!

5. God wants to step sovereignly into our world again.

It doesn't matter what you call it: revival, outpouring, renewal, visitation, or awakening. Historically and biblically His presence with accompanied power has invaded our world many times in the past and brought correction to both the church and the culture. Due to our lack of success in leading the church through natural leadership, we desperately need Him to step into our world again. The God who loves His creation and has the power to do whatever it takes to get His work done is looking for supernatural leaders who will allow His kingdom to come and invade our natural environment.

Do I Really Believe What I Say About Him?

One of the greatest challenges we face on this journey is to take an honest look at what we know about God and ask one simple question: Do I really believe it?

Is He really omnipresent?

Do we really believe that God is in all places at one time? Is He always where I am, and is He always where everyone else is?

Is He really omniscient?

Do we really believe that God knows everything that there is to be known? Does He fully know all of my thoughts and all of what is in my heart? Does He know what is in everyone's heart?

Is He really omnipotent?

Do we really believe that God has immeasurable power that is only limited by His own constraints as to when and how He wants to use it?

Do we really believe what He says about Himself in Scripture?

Is He really the God of perfect mercy, justice, grace, love, and patience? Is He really a God who is capable and willing to do what He says He will?

For those of us in vocational ministry, how we view our call and purpose can vary from person to person. Yet personally, I'm not sure why any of us would give ourselves to a ministry call if we don't believe God is who He says He is. How can we ever hope to effect lasting change in the lives of our people if He isn't?

There is another aspect of this process of assessing what we believe that can't be missed. You see, if we struggle to embrace that God is always present, has unlimited power, knows everything that there is to be known, and is who He says He is, then we will struggle to take the risks necessary to move into another dimension of church leadership. How could a person even begin to consider stepping into the arena of supernatural leadership unless God is omnipotent, omniscient, and omnipresent? That's the wonderful reality of where this brings us. He is, so we can!

Supernatural leadership is a leadership journey that demands stepping out without a safety net to catch us. Our plan "B" is:

"Go back to plan A because He is able." Does this type of leadership demand perfection? Is there no grace for human error in supernatural leadership? No, it doesn't demand perfection and yes, there is grace for error. This is the beauty of supernatural leadership. We don't have to build and create our own back-up safety net. He is our net! Believe me, God is quite able to catch us if we fall.

If you find it difficult to trust Him, then operating in natural leadership is where you will stay. In natural leadership you can calculate your moves and manage your risks. On the other hand, if you are determined to become a supernatural leader, it's not about calculating. It's about obeying. It's not about managing, it's about relating.

Look around you. There are needs in our world that:

- Great planning cannot meet
- Great education cannot meet
- Great money cannot meet
- Great systems cannot meet

This is where supernatural leadership can make a difference.

Chapter 6
LET'S GET JESUS
INTO THE PICTURE

NINA'S FATHER ESCAPED from Russia during WWII, and after the war he made his way to the United States. He never returned to Russia until 1988, when we persuaded him to go with us on a trip into the then communist Soviet Union. I had served active duty in the U.S. Army, and a few years prior to the trip to the Soviet Union, I had resigned my commission as an officer in the Illinois National Guard. In that season, President Reagan had introduced his Star Wars defense plan, and the Soviets were absolutely beside themselves with the U.S.

Our three-city tour of Leningrad (St. Petersburg), Kiev, and Moscow, began in Leningrad. On our first morning after arrival, we boarded a tour bus that took us to a beautiful city square. I don't remember much about the square itself. All that my memory logged was what the square was filled with that day—hundreds of Soviet soldiers. It was the week before May Day, and they were rehearsing for the annual May Day military parade. Words cannot describe the flood of emotions I felt walking through the square and literally rubbing shoulders with what I as an American soldier had known as "the enemy."

If this is how I felt after entering a moment of "I can't believe I'm experiencing this," I cannot imagine what emotions Jesus must have experienced when, as Creator of the universe, He entered into a culture hostile to His presence here on earth. When Jesus appeared on the scene, not only were things not well with humanity as a whole, but they specifically were not well for the Jews. Let's look at the environment in which He walked out His destiny as we paint Jesus into our new picture of leadership.

For hundreds of years prior to Jesus' birth, Jerusalem and the Jews were under the authority of several different occupying nations. During the time of His earthly life, Jerusalem and Israel were under Roman rule. Other occupiers had allowed Israel to self-govern under their authority through the High Priests. This was still the case in Jesus' day.

The role of the High Priest was meant to be spiritual at its inception, but it now reflected its culture. Instead of standing between God and His people, the High Priests were now rulers of people "just like all the other nations." After many years of occupation, they were ready for the Messiah. What was it that they were looking for from their Messiah? An earthly king— "just like all the other nations."

Jesus' Leadership Model

Even though Jesus was rejected as Messiah when He didn't fit their criteria, He walked out His leadership in a very tenuous environment. He had to walk in three cultures at the same time. Those three cultures were the kingdom of God, the Jewish culture, and the Roman culture. Let's look at some examples of how He handled Himself. Remember, this is God in the flesh, living out leadership the way it was meant to be expressed. We need to pay very close attention to this.

> Truly, truly, I say to you, he who believes in Me, the works that I do, he will do also; and greater works than these he will do; because I go to the Father.
>
> —JOHN 14:12

When Jesus uses the phrase "the works that I do, he will do also," He is clearly communicating that He is living His life as a demonstration to all of us who want to follow Him. That is what this chapter is all about. We are not only asking the question, "What did Jesus do?" in terms of leadership, but "How did He do it?" This will by no means be an exhaustive study, but an overview for laying our new foundation. After you begin to recognize His supernatural leadership, you will see it constantly throughout the gospels.

> Then some Pharisees and scribes came to Jesus from Jerusalem and said, "Why do Your disciples break the tradition of the elders? For they do not wash their hands when they eat bread." And He said to them, "Why do you yourselves transgress the commandment of God for the sake of your tradition?"
>
> —MATTHEW 15:1–3

This is just one of many encounters that Jesus had with the Pharisees. We might say that they often "butted heads." What we can take from these encounters is that Jesus never allowed them to alter His course. They didn't understand His leadership; they were threatened by it. No matter what approach they tried to use to shift Him, He never gave an inch. How could He do that? He knew what the truth was, and was committed to not giving up that territory. He was also demonstrating supernatural leadership freedom, which the Pharisees who only understood control, despised.

> As Jesus went on from there, two blind men followed Him, crying out, "Have mercy on us, Son of David!" When He entered the house, the blind men came up to Him, and Jesus said to them, "Do you believe that I am able to do this?" They said to Him, "Yes, Lord." Then He touched their eyes saying, "It shall be done to you according to your faith."
>
> —MATTHEW 9:27–29

As a person with a task-oriented, driven personality, I love this aspect of Jesus' leadership. His life had "flow." When something unplanned or unscripted came up, He never reacted to it as an intrusion on His life. He held every moment and every situation as an opportunity for the kingdom to invade someone's life through Him. No complaint, no rolling of the eyes, and no pushing people away. He flowed with the conviction that the Father was instrumental in all of His daily events.

> Then the mother of the sons of Zebedee came to Jesus with her sons, bowing down and making a request of Him. And He said to her, "What do you wish?" She said to Him, "Command that in Your kingdom these two sons of mine may sit one on Your right and one on your left".... But Jesus called them to Himself and said, "You know that the rulers of the Gentiles lord it over them, and their great men exercise authority over them. It is not this way among you, but whoever wishes to become great among you shall be your servant, and whoever wishes to be first among you shall be your slave."
>
> —Matthew 20:20–21, 25–27

On a number of occasions, people asked things of Jesus that had something to do with their standing or position. As a supernatural leader, He didn't evaluate the possibilities and give them their "odds" for success at receiving what they wanted. He didn't interview them in order to assess their giftings or natural qualifications. Instead He pointed them to a higher value and standing, the position of their heart. It wasn't always appreciated by those who petitioned Him (i.e. the rich young ruler), but he attempted to shift their eyes from personal gain to the higher value of kingdom gain.

> Carry no money belt, no bag, no shoes; and greet no one on the way.
>
> —Luke 10:4

As a mentor of supernatural leadership to the disciples, Jesus called them to step outside of their comfort zone. The natural man reasons that if you are going to be traveling over an extended journey, then you are going to need to bring along provisions sufficient for the trip. On this occasion Jesus tells them not to take any provisions along. This is a pivotal moment for their development. It is time for them to experience supernatural provision from the Father. It is a key revelation for all who aspire to this leadership. The disciples are about to discover that Father God will take care of them, even when they are away from the watchful eyes of Jesus. This is the day that they are weaned from natural thinking, and move into the joy and delight of supernatural provision. Once they understand that He is capable of caring for them in any situation, they are free to go anywhere, anytime, to do anything He calls them to do.

> Now as they were traveling along, He entered a village; and a woman named Martha welcomed Him into her home. She had a sister called Mary, who was seated at the Lord's feet, listening to His word…"but only one thing is necessary, for Mary has chosen the good part, which shall not be taken away from her."
> —LUKE 10:38–39, 42

This is so big. When Jesus taught, men sat at His feet to receive instruction from the "Rabbi." Culturally with the Jews, Mary was sitting in a place that women had been forbidden to occupy. We often get caught up in the Martha vs. Mary war in the story and miss an important message. What Jesus has done here, by affirming Mary's place at His feet with the men, is to affirm the place of women in the kingdom.

Wow! This Gospel story isn't just about which is better, doing or being. It is about a woman who steps into a culturally and religiously forbidden arena, and finds herself in the welcoming presence of Jesus. Yes, religion with its rules and barriers was in disbelief. Jesus models a supernatural leadership that doesn't push people away or keep them behind invisible walls. Instead, He affirms people, sets them free, and levels the field for all.

> When they came to Capernaum, those who collected the two-drachma tax came to Peter and said, "Does your teacher not pay the two-drachma tax?" He said, "Yes." And when he came into the house, Jesus spoke to him first, saying, "What do you think, Simon? From whom do the kings of the earth collect customs or poll-tax, from their sons or from strangers?" When Peter said, "From strangers," Jesus said to him, "Then the sons are exempt. However, so that we do not offend them, go to the sea and throw in a hook, and take the first fish that comes up; and when you open its mouth, you will find a shekel. Take that and give it to them for you and Me."
>
> —MATTHEW 17:24–27

The Jewish authorities were demanding payment of Jesus' personal temple tax. Isn't this a great picture? Taxing the Messiah for His own temple tax! Watch here what He does. In order to pay His legal obligation, He sends Peter out to do something that Peter knew so well. How many times prior to this occasion do you think Peter had caught a fish with a coin in its mouth? You've got it. None. He is teaching Peter an invaluable supernatural lesson here. When Peter casts his line out to catch a fish, in the natural it looks like he is casting it into the world of water and fish. In reality, he is casting it into the other real world, the kingdom of heaven. As he pulls in his line, he is literally pulling in miraculous provision from the unseen kingdom of heaven, and drawing it into the natural realm. From this day forward Peter understood what I am imparting into you: a supernatural leader is backed up by a reality of greater resources than the world we live in. We simply need to reach out, take hold of it, and pull it into our situation!

> Therefore Jesus answered and was saying to them, "Truly, truly, I say to you, the Son can do nothing of Himself, unless it is something He sees the Father doing; for whatever the Father does, these things the Son also does in like manner. For the Father loves the Son, and shows Him all things that He Himself is doing; and the Father will show Him greater works that these, so that you will marvel."
>
> —JOHN 5:19–20

Here is where Jesus' success at leadership has its basis. It is directly linked to His relationship with the Father. Out of that open relationship Jesus has access to information that guides Him through each day.

Let's stop and consider for a moment the implications of that statement. How many of us wouldn't like to have more insight into the arenas that we have responsibility for? If we could just have additional perspective on how we should proceed with what is in front of us, we know that we could improve our level of successful leadership. That is exactly what Jesus is trying to get across to us. It is possible to get that revelation, when you spend time with Father God. If you could picture it in your mind, this is the place where Jesus holds up the master key and says, "Pay attention. This is what you are looking for. It is the key that unlocks doors that separate the natural and the supernatural realms. If you want to move from natural leadership to supernatural leadership, you will need this key."

Take another look at what Jesus is conveying with this passage. When asked about how He is able to accomplish the things He does, Jesus responds by telling them that "of Himself" or *in the natural*, He can't. Wait a minute! Here is a man who has spent a vast portion of His life in the synagogue and temple, listening to, teaching, and receiving some of life's best training. He is saying that even though He has been equipped and trained to lead and influence others; that training didn't have the ability to allow Him to move at the level of authority that He was demonstrating. He is pointing us to His source, an intimate relationship with Father God. Look closely and you will see Jesus standing by a large sign reading, "This is the way!" Can you see it?

> Nathanael said to him, "Can any good thing come out of Nazareth?" Philip said to him, "Come and see." Jesus saw Nathanael coming to Him, and said of him, "Behold, an Israelite indeed, in whom there is no deceit." Nathanael said to Him, "How do You know me?" Jesus answered and said to him, "Before Philip called you, when you were under the fig tree, I saw you."
>
> —John 1:46–48

Jesus made a significant impact on Nathanael when He spoke about seeing him at a specific location, even though Nathanael knew that Jesus had not physically been there. Nathanael had an early leadership "experience" with Jesus. Even though Nathanael was a *doubter* in relation to the value of being called to come meet Jesus by Philip, Jesus didn't try to sell Nathanael on the concept of following Him. He didn't meet Nathanael with "Let me share my vision statement with you. I am about to build something here and I'm going to give you a chance to be a part of it from the ground up." All Jesus had to do was tell Nathanael of a vision that He had of him, and he was ready to follow Jesus anywhere.

Jesus demonstrated the power of supernatural revelation to bring people into an experience that will set them free to step into their destiny. Natural leaders are visionary concerning the future, but supernatural leaders see visions of the present as well.

Every day Jesus was living out theocracy before the disciples and others. He was demonstrating that when you know the Father, spend time with Him, and follow Him, things happen bigger than humanly possible. "With *man* this is impossible, but with *God* all things are possible" (Matt. 19:26, NIV). We see that He wasn't just offering mankind access to God's love and power. He was demonstrating and offering us access to the kingdom of heaven as well.

What Happened After Jesus Left?

After pouring the kingdom into the disciples for over three years, and demonstrating to them what happens when God is allowed to be in charge, what did they do with it? At the outset they implemented the values that Jesus modeled.

> So they put forward two men, Joseph called Barsabbas (who was also called Justus), and Matthias. And they prayed and said, "You, Lord, who know the hearts of all men, show which one of these two You have chosen to occupy this ministry and apostleship from which Judas turned aside to go to his own place." And they drew lots for them, and the lot fell to Matthias, and he was added to the eleven apostles.
>
> —ACTS 1:23–26

Here we see them look to the Father for direction, and use the casting of lots as a means for Him to influence the outcome. Whatever level of personal revelation they had on supernatural leadership, history shows that they were not successful at passing it on to those that they raised up. As the apostles died, a gradual shift toward institutionalization of the church began. There were two factors that contributed to this end.

First of all, the church was under growing persecution from the state. The response to persecution often is to do what early American settlers would do when under attack. They would circle the wagons in order to protect themselves from outside aggression. Once the wagons have been circled, all forward movement stops. It is no longer about moving into or taking new territory, it is only about survival.

Secondly, there was also a lot of heretical teaching being given. One of the best ways to deal with people who are expressing something you don't like is to shut them out. A conventional way to do that is to create an institution for the "us" camp, and not allow "them" to join.

These two situations laid the foundation for organizing and institutionalizing the church. When Constantine converted to Christianity in A.D. 312, it became the final "nail in the coffin" for any remnant left of Jesus' model of theocracy. Constantine issued the Edict of Milan in A.D. 313 that resulted in him becoming actively involved in the direction of the church. From that day to the present, the New Testament church has been built not on theocracy, but on systems, structure, and programs as a means of existence and expansion. It's who we are, what we do and how we have functioned as the church. We have obviously gotten relatively good at it. After all, we have been practicing it for several thousand years.

Theocracy that is dependent upon supernatural leadership was God's original plan. If it is what Jesus walked in and modeled for us, then it is within our reach. Supernatural leadership is accessible and attainable. He does not call us to a place that we cannot reach.

In the same sense, He does not take us to greater places of satisfaction unless we are unsatisfied with where we are. How about you? Have you grown tired of natural leadership with its natural fruit? Is there something alive in you that is beginning to grow? Can you feel it, but not find words to describe it? It's the image of Christ beginning to renew your mind and heart. You are just beginning, and it gets better. A lot better.

Chapter 7
CONTRASTING COLORS

I HAVE A CONFESSION to make. To my wife's chagrin, I have a difficult time distinguishing between navy blue and black. It has not been uncommon to sit down with a group of people, cross my legs, and reveal that I have navy blue socks on, with my black slacks. It's not a pretty sight. In the closet where I pick out my clothes, they both look the same to me until it becomes revealed in the light sometime later. Even in normal light, navy blue looks black to me until it is held in contrast to black. When put side by side, I can see the difference.

In this chapter we are going to put natural leadership and supernatural leadership side by side so that you can see the difference. Some things are understood best when held in contrast. For some of you, it has been a challenge to see the difference to this point.

Before we look at the contrasts between natural leadership and supernatural leadership, I want to take a moment to take another look with you at natural leadership. When I refer to natural leadership, I will also often refer to systems, processes, and structure. My concern with systems, processes, and structure is not that they should not exist when we are working toward building the church. The human body is evidence that systems, processes, and structure are essential in order for individual parts to successfully accomplish something bigger than themselves. In the same way, as I stated in chapter one, natural leadership has a definite role in building up the leader's toolbox for the work that is ahead. It is not the existence of natural leadership, or systems, processes, and structure that is my greatest concern. What I am challenging in this book is our dependence on natural leadership, systems, processes, and structure.

Contrasting the Two Leadership Models

Natural leadership depends on my efforts. Supernatural leadership depends on God for the results.

The natural leadership model spends its energy and focus on development. That development is of systems, structure, procedures, and methods. All of that is hinged on the development of the leader. The success of the leader's effort is dependent upon a number of factors that all involve the level of the leader's ability.

A supernatural leader recognizes that natural limitations can keep them from being as effective as they have a heart to be. Therefore, they press into Him to get His strategy for their situation. While walking out His strategy, they are quite attuned to the fact that success will only come if His hand moves into that arena.

Most of you have a personal vehicle. What did it take for the manufacturer to get that vehicle assembled? Each part had to be precisely designed and manufactured. Those parts were then shipped to one location, and placed together in a predetermined order. Your vehicle is a tribute to the power of human ingenuity. It is a marvel. When you go to get into your car, start the engine, and travel down the street, it is because hundreds, if not thousands, of people worked together to pull it off. That is the picture of natural leadership. Basically, if we can figure it out, we can do it.

Now picture in your mind a simple, small rug that you have somewhere around your home. It could be at the entrance door, kitchen, or bathroom. If you were to sit down on that rug and it were to begin to travel where you wanted it to go, now that would be supernatural!

The car is a testimony to the greatness of man. The flying rug would be a testimony of the greatness of God. The supernatural leader on the carpet knows that "this thing won't fly unless He shows up." Though I don't anticipate that any of us will ever have the experience of riding on a flying rug, this illustrates the dynamic difference between the two approaches.

Natural leadership depends on hard work and development of skills. Supernatural leadership depends on the person's willingness to listen to and follow Father God.

There is nothing wrong with hard work. We were made to be productive, not lazy. On the other hand, I hate doing things the hard way, especially if I know that there is an easier way for it to be done. Across the board, one of the greatest challenges most pastors face is that we are too busy to spend time with God. What are we busy doing? We are busy planning, building, or fixing our many local church systems and structures.

I recently attended a Christian marketplace leadership conference. To my surprise, a nationally known motivational speaker told us all to loudly proclaim, "It's all about me!" They went on to explain that the reason we were to proclaim that phrase was to emphasize that our success was dependent upon us. They were simply unmasking the heart of natural leadership—it's all about me. If *I* can acquire a certain level of skills, then *I* should be able to see *my* success. Again, is the development of these skills wrong? No. But it is wrong when achieving success is all about me.

Supernatural leaders know that if they spend time building a relationship with the Father, several important things will happen. First, He reveals His strategies. Secondly, He strengthens and encourages His servant. Thirdly, He sovereignly moves and shifts things around on behalf of His servant/friend. Valerie, a ministry friend of mine, recently exclaimed this revelation to me: "It's amazing what the Lord will tell you when you spend time with Him!" In the end, it is all about Him, not about me.

Let's go back to the words of Samuel to Israel, when they wanted a king to lead them instead of God.

> He will also take your daughters for perfumers and cooks and bakers. He will take the best of your fields and your vineyards and your olive groves and give them to his servants. He will take a tenth of your seed and of your vineyards and give to his officers and to his servants. He will also take your male servants and your female servants and your best young men and your donkeys and use them for his work. He will take a tenth of your flocks, and you yourselves will become his servants.
>
> —1 Samuel 8:13–17

From its inception, the success of natural leadership has come from its ability to take from those that are under its leadership. This is a tough one to look at.

The scripture we just looked at indicates that when you don't have theocracy, and humans are empowered to lead by their own abilities, they achieve their goals of leadership by taking from those they lead. Now honestly, what have we been doing for generations in our churches? For the most part, we equip and lead people into places where we can use them so that we can build a successful ministry. In a very subtle way, we take from them in order to meet our goals and vision. I don't need to belabor the point. You have the picture. Lord, have mercy.

Natural leadership is a model that depends on the performance of others. Supernatural leadership's focus is on relationships that set people free to use their gifts.

Since it is true that no leaders are islands unto themselves, leaders understand the value of equipping those that they are dependent upon for the success of their mission. Natural leaders must select, move, posture, train, and motivate those who will be instrumental in accomplishing their goals. This is the basic role of all leaders. In order for the church to move forward toward achieving its goals, the natural leader must get people into the needed positions. If those people fail to measure up to the level of performance expected of them, meeting the goal is in jeopardy.

Supernatural leadership flows out of the spirit of freedom. The leader invests into ministry relationships with the goal of helping individuals discover both their giftings and their destiny. There are no clones being made here. Individuals are empowered and encouraged to discover that God wants to do powerful and significant things through them. The supernatural leader isn't interested in taking from those they lead, because they understand that through training and releasing there will be a much greater progression of kingdom expansion. When God's power begins moving through these people, the leader won't have to be concerned with motivating them, as they are serving a higher cause than that of accomplishing their leader's agenda.

Let's take this topic and bring Jesus into it. We all know that Jesus spent His three final years in teaching and training His followers. Do we see any evidence that after training them, that He used them for His personal gain or to advance His own agenda? It is just not there.

Natural leadership, with its systems, often places leaders in a place of being controlled by others. Supernatural leadership allows the leader to be free of control or manipulation of others.

There have been volumes of books written, churches split, resignations written, and buckets of tears shed over this natural leadership arrangement. In most natural leadership scenarios, the pastor/spiritual leader has a group of empowered people that heavily influence the decisions the organization makes. Here just about every plate that the pastor is spinning on the end of a stick (the systems and structure that they are managing) is under the watchful scrutiny of a few. The stress and emotional bondage can be overwhelming. In most situations the natural leader resigns to the realization that this is just the way ministry is.

A supernatural leader is in an environment where people are free to follow the direction and revelation that they receive out of relationship with the Father. They are free to take risks that may be unconventional, and they also set those under their leadership free to experience the same. The supernatural leader also sets those under his leadership free to experience the same. Here both leaders and followers are allowed to make mistakes and receive grace from others involved.

> Laban said, "Good, let it be according to your word." So he removed on that day the striped and spotted male goats and all the speckled and spotted female goats, every one with white in it, and all the black ones among the sheep, and gave them into the care of his sons. And he put a distance of three days' journey between himself and Jacob, and Jacob fed the rest of Laban's flocks. Then Jacob took fresh rods of poplar and almond and plane trees, and peeled white stripes in them, exposing the white which was in the rods. He set the rods which he had peeled in front of the flocks in the gutters, even in the watering troughs, where the flocks came to drink; and they mated when they came to drink. So the flocks mated by the rods, and the flocks brought forth striped, speckled, and spotted.
>
> —Genesis 30:34–39

> When He had finished speaking, He said to Simon, "Put out into the deep water and let down your nets for a catch." Simon answered and said, "Master, we worked hard all night and caught nothing, but I will do as You

say and let down the nets." When they had done this, they enclosed a great quantity of fish, and their nets began to break.

—LUKE 5:4–6

A supernatural leader learns to hear and obey in faith what may not make sense. This step opens the door for God-sized results. Both Jacob and Simon Peter experienced the reality of what God is able to do, even when they were asked to do something unconventional or illogical. Natural leaders often do not even consider the possibility of walking in this place, because they know that those empowered around them would never set them free to take such risks.

Natural leadership expects leaders to do the "dirty work" for those they lead. Supernatural leadership points people to personal responsibility.

Natural leaders wear a mantle that is very fatiguing. It is the mantle that makes them personally responsible for the welfare of everyone they lead. And it began the day Israel shifted from theocracy to self rule:

> "…that we also may be like all the nations, that our king may judge us and go out before us and fight our battles."

—1 SAMUEL 8:20

What they expected of their leader was that he "may go out before us and fight our battles." This is exactly how much of the local church views the role of the pastor. The leader is expected to fight their congregational and personal battles for them. Natural leaders wear the weight of responsibility to ensure that their people are at rest and at peace. Can it be done? Not successfully, but we keep trying with all of the ability we can muster.

Supernatural leaders teach and train their people to develop their own relationship with Father God. Out of that relationship they learn that God alone is both their source and peace. Supernatural leaders bring their people into an understanding of their personal responsibility for life choices and destiny. Here the leader isn't unnecessarily encumbered with the responsibility of fighting everyone's battles for them. The supernatural leader empowers people to take on their own battles, which in the end allows them to be able to celebrate their own God victories.

In the end, the difference between the two approaches is simple. In natural leadership, a person is looked to for strategy and effort in order to win a victory. In supernatural leadership, God Himself is looked to for strategy and effort for the victory. I know which one I would rather have working on my behalf.

Natural leadership is dependent upon intelligence and education. Supernatural leadership requires an inner brilliance.

One need only look at the pastoral training process in the United States to see how highly we value education. We have a sense that if we will just get the right training we will be able to lead successfully. Natural leadership dictates that any shortcoming of our performance stems from either not being properly trained, or not applying what we have been trained. There are a lot of very intelligent men and women leading God's people. On the other hand, if the kingdom of God is really dependent upon our intelligence, then the kingdom is in some real trouble.

Even though training is essential for a supernatural leader, this leader understands that a brilliance of the life of God's Spirit in them is of greater value. A supernatural leader understands the implication of this text:

> For consider your calling, brethren, that there were not many wise according to the flesh, not many mighty, not many noble; but God has chosen the foolish things of the world to shame the wise, and God has chosen the

weak things of the world to shame the things which are strong, and the base things of the world and the despised God has chosen, the things that are not, so that He may nullify the things that are, so that no man may boast before God.

—1 CORINTHIANS 1:26–29

Those of you who are still embracing natural leadership may be feeling really defensive about your investment into your education. You don't need to be defensive. Education and natural wisdom can be a good thing. However, according to the verses that we just looked at, God is operating from a different set of priorities. I'm going to go with His priorities. Here is another way of putting this. A natural leader pursues knowledge that is based on the experience and understanding of others. A supernatural leader pursues knowledge of what God is doing and saying for their given situations.

Brightening the Color of Supernatural Leadership

Outside of the contrasts that we have just looked at, the supernatural leader is much more.

A supernatural leader is a follower first. It will never work for a person to walk in supernatural leadership if they have not developed a follower's heart. Since supernatural leadership is dependent upon the leader's willingness to constantly say "yes, Lord" to His direction, the independent spirit cannot live or thrive here.

A supernatural leader is a bridge-builder. Here the heart of the leader is not given to building and protecting their "territory." The supernatural leader moves to bring down walls and barriers that divide the body of Christ. Bridges of relationship are built with others so that mutual support and encouragement can be shared with one another.

Supernatural leaders are kingdom-builders. Their focus is not to become famous and be "rulers over many." Their energy isn't invested into what they can get out of ministry. Supernatural leaders know they are called to build God's kingdom, not their own.

A supernatural leader is a risk-taker. This cannot be avoided. The realm of the supernatural functions in a different reality than the natural world we live in. When we exercise natural leadership, we measure, plan, and calculate the processes based on known natural laws and principles. The unseen kingdom of heaven operates outside of our natural limitations. A supernatural leader must be willing to take the risks that the Father calls them to, in order to bring supernatural manifestation into this reality. Jesus demonstrated this from time to time with things like mud and spit placed on blind eyes, pots filled with water before becoming wine, and five loaves and two fish being passed around to feed thousands.

A supernatural leader removes boxes and restores freedom. In the Garden of Eden, God only communicated one restriction to Adam and Eve: don't eat the fruit from one tree. Picture in your mind a white sheet of poster board. In the middle, place a ¼ inch by ¼ inch box to represent this one restriction. This little box on a large blank poster board is a visual picture of the freedom Adam and Eve were given. In essence, "You can go anywhere and do anything you want, just leave the little box alone." So what happens next? They violate their one restriction, and God gives them more restrictions. Take a moment and place some more boxes on that imaginary poster board.

By the time Jesus comes to dwell here, that poster is literally covered with some of God's restrictions and a whole bunch of man's restrictions. Self-rule has a way of developing rules and restrictions for people. To put it plainly, it is called "control." In order to get people to do what leaders want them to do, leaders create boxes and tell people what they can and can't do. This is where Jesus drove the Pharisee's absolutely mad. We are all familiar with Jesus walking through the walls after His resurrection to meet with the disciples. Before walking through natural walls, Jesus got some practice while He was alive at walking through the walls and boxes that self-rule had created.

> "Why do Your disciples break the tradition of the elders? For they do not wash their hands when they eat bread."
> —Matthew 15:2

> At that time Jesus went through the grainfields on the Sabbath, and His disciples became hungry and began to pick the heads of grain and eat. But when the Pharisees saw this, they said to Him, "Look, Your disciples do what is not lawful to do on the Sabbath."
> —Matthew 12:1–2

Supernatural leaders remove boxes that hinder the movement, growth, and maturity of those they lead. Supernatural leaders, like Jesus, have the Father's perspective as to what rules and restrictions are healthy for their people, and which ones are pointless, out of season, and needlessly adding burdens on their people. They understand the value of safety, but also the value of freedom.

A supernatural leader understands that he/she will experience pain. This pain will come from a number of sources. Sometimes it will be the pain of walking away from long-term relationships. (I'm not referring to your marriage here.) Whenever we lose the ability to be free, it is time to walk away. Sometimes it will be the pain of disappointment. Even though supernatural leadership is God's plan, things don't always work out the way we expect them to. We don't always "hit the ball over the fence," so to speak. There will be strikeouts along the way. The supernatural leader knows that it is better to strike out than to never get up to the plate. This is where we assess our loss and learn from it, but most importantly we don't give up. We march right back up to the plate when we have the next opportunity.

A supernatural leader is a childlike leader. Becoming a supernatural leader really does mean that many of us will have to "unlearn" a lot of what we have been taught and modeled. The Father wants to work with leaders who have the heart of a child. Along with the aspect of simple trust that children have toward authority, there are a couple of other key factors. First, children never complicate issues. Life is very simple to them. Supernatural leaders don't need to understand everything. They just need to simply follow His instruction and rest in its outcome. Secondly, children have a sense that everything is going to come together in the end. Children pick up on things that we adults are too consumed to be able to perceive. A supernatural leader watches with fascination as God sovereignly orchestrates a beautiful outcome.

A supernatural leader makes room for miracles to happen. Some of you may have been processing how you would like to become a supernatural leader as long as nothing "weird" happens. This could be a problem. You see, supernatural leadership is about cooperating with the Lord's Prayer. Remember the part about "Your kingdom come, Your will be done"?

When His kingdom comes into your world, something is going to happen. A sickness is going to be healed. An afflicted mind will be set free. A marriage will be restored. Abundant life will flow in relationships. Laughter will flow. An angel could show up. Whatever He chooses to do, He will do it. However He chooses to express His presence, He is free to express it. Don't forget the basics. God is good, very good. I guarantee you, what He brings with Him when His kingdom comes, is going to be good!

The fact that God does the miraculous (and that He still does it today) is a strong rationale for supernatural leadership. Our whole motivation is that the challenges we face are greater than our personal and collective natural abilities to be able to handle them. A supernatural leader is looking and praying for God to invade his territory so that God-sized fruit and impact is the product of their leadership journey.

Though I have been spending time to build a rational and biblical case for supernatural leadership; for a leader to step into the supernatural, it takes more than reasoning. When Jesus began His ministry, one of the first things He did was to call together those that he had chosen to disciple. When Jesus came up to some of them He simply said:

> "Follow Me, and I will make you become fishers of men."
>
> —MARK 1:17

No details. No debates. No long discussions about the ramifications of His offer. With just one brief invitation they walked away from everything they had known, to pursue something that they didn't fully understand. How is it that they could do that? It was because Jesus wasn't appealing to their intellect. He was appealing to their hearts. Their hearts said, "Yes, I must do this."

What is your heart hearing? Is He calling you to step into supernatural leadership? I can't answer that for you. You have to own that decision for yourself.

Chapter 8
CREATING A NEW IMAGE

ONE OF THE things that I have enjoyed about this season of my life is that a few years ago I received my private pilot's license. If you were able to look at my face each time I come off of the runway, you would probably see me smiling.

Presently I am learning to fly a different model of plane than the one that I was originally trained on. To do that, you have to fly with a flight instructor until they are confident in your ability to safely handle the plane on your own. When you are being trained, and when you are flying with another licensed pilot beside you, there is often a transfer back and forth of the controls of the plane. One example of that would be when an instructor wants to demonstrate a maneuver. At that point, they take over the maneuvering of the plane with the controls at the right-seat side. In order to keep confusion from happening during the transfer of responsibility from one pilot to the other, the FAA has instructed that specific phrases be used. The pilot in command says to the co-pilot, "You have the plane." The co-pilot responds with, "I have the plane." The process is to repeat itself each time control of the plane is transferred. Even though the FAA has figured out a way for pilots to clearly and safely transfer control, it is not always so easy for church leaders.

By now you may have figured out that natural leadership is all about being in control. In that same sense it is also about how successful we are at being able to control our environment. Supernatural leaders know that they have a responsibility to develop the skills to "fly the plane." What makes them different is that they are quick to release control when their Yahweh co-pilot says, "I want the plane now." Supernatural leaders have no problem with the response, "You have the plane."

It's a new picture of leadership that we are developing here. Now is the time for us to put the finishing touches on the image of supernatural leadership that covers our canvas.

It's Time for a New Wineskin

> "Nor do people put new wine into old wineskins; other-wise the wineskins burst, and the wine pours out and the wineskins are ruined; but they put new wine into fresh wineskins, and both are preserved."
> —MATTHEW 9:17

The church is in real need of the new wineskin of super-natural leadership. In the process of developing supernatural leadership, the wisdom of Matthew 9:17 must be adhered to. If you try to take supernatural leadership and make it fit into the old model of systems, structures, and human effort, the journey can be quite frustrating and potentially destructive.

Why frustrating? Because supernatural leadership operates at a high level of freedom. Its ability to flow, shift, and respond when God says, "Move!" is its primary dynamic. For those of you who are in church situations that have traditional systems set up for generations, let me both caution and encourage you. The caution I extend to you is to not expect to bring about any substantial shift from natural leadership to supernatural lead-ership in a short period of time. Forcing a shift could become very destructive to a church, and you were not called to destroy it, but to build it up. I do want to encourage you to personally press into supernatural leadership, while operating within the leadership system that you have. I believe that as you walk in the levels of supernatural leadership where you have authority, God will confirm His hand on you with your people, which in turn will release greater opportunities for transformation.

In this picture of wine and wineskins, I would like to bring clarity to the roles each one plays. The new wine is the kingdom of God that is supernatural, powerful, alive, and being poured out on the church. Of course, the wineskin is the church at large—or the body of Christ. The ability for the church body to contain the new wine has everything to do with its leadership.

For those of you who have studied or researched church history, you will know that there have been seasons of revival or outpourings. In these seasons, the Spirit of God moved upon people in specific locations at specific times. New wine was poured out and God-sized transformation would occur. Whether it be the Welsh revivals, Argentine revival, Great Awakening, Cane Ridge, Azusa Street, Toronto, or Pensacola revival, around the world God has at times stepped in and revealed Himself as the God of the impossible. He has visited His people because we have called upon Him, and because He knows how badly we need His presence to help us.

When we look at the condition of America and the condition of the church, we again realize that unless He comes to empower His church, America will continue to pursue its passion to destroy itself through immorality, addictions, and rebellion. We need Him to pour out His new wine upon us again. We need Him to arrest the hearts of both saint and sinner with His love, mercy, and grace. We need for His kingdom to come in power, just as it came through Jesus' ministry 2,000 years ago.

Not only do we "need" Him to send revival, renewal, outpouring, or awakening again, but I am convinced that He is about to do just that. This time I believe that He is waiting for something to happen here on earth first. Before He pours out His new wine all over the earth in these last days, He is waiting for the formation of the new wineskin. This new wineskin will have a supernatural leadership that can stretch with His presence. A leadership that is alive with possibilities and willing to take the risks to do what the Father is doing.

What have been the results in most situations, when the living, breathing, expanding, new wine of His presence came to churches that are constrained by structures and systems? Over time the pressure on the old skin caused it to be spilled out. When it spills out, the power of God is diminished, people lose interest, churches can be divided, and it is officially labeled a past event in history.

The supernatural was never made to be contained, controlled, or managed by the natural. When God shows up, natural leadership responds like Peter on the Mount of Transfiguration.

> And He was transfigured before them; and His face shone like the sun, and His garments became as white as light. And behold, Moses and Elijah appeared to them, talking with Him. Peter said to Jesus, "Lord, it is good for us to be here; if You wish, I will make three tabernacles here, one for You, and one for Moses, and one for Elijah."
> —Matthew 17:2–4

What a great natural response Peter demonstrates. The first thing we always want to do when God shows up is to *build something!* We want to build things like buildings, create events, direct the environment, and promote ourselves. That isn't to say that there shouldn't be something built, but the direction needs to come from the Father, not conventional leadership knowledge that is modeled after its culture. The natural leadership wineskin wants to be able to keep everything under control. It doesn't like surprises and it doesn't like to be made uncomfortable.

Just step back with me for a moment and take a logical look at this. The things of the kingdom of heaven were meant from the beginning to be released on earth through theocratic leaders.

Since the church leadership system has been modeled after our culture, it is no wonder that it is not capable of sustaining an outpouring of the kingdom over a long period of time. It was not made to and it cannot.

Right now the Father is looking for supernatural leaders who will allow Him to use them to build new church leadership wineskins, so that when He pours out His new wine it will be sustained not for weeks, months or years, but for generations. Supernatural leadership is the key to unlocking leadership for all future generations. Supernatural leadership is the key to restoration of God's powerful influence on the earth.

Transitioning into the New Wineskin

To my knowledge, God rarely makes any of us become something that we don't want to be or aren't interested in. The same principle holds true with becoming supernatural leaders. It has to be pursued. It is something that you have to be hungry for personally. You have to go after it and surrender yourself to it.

Becoming a supernatural leadership wineskin requires us to give up our fascination with titles.

If we are obsessed with the achievement of being known by a title, we need to let it go. Under theocracy, prior to the anointing of Saul as king, no one that God used had a title. Moses, Abraham, Isaac, Jacob—none had a title. They were *just* men willing to let God use them to lead others. If supernatural leadership appeals to you as a way to get into the spotlight, you have entirely missed the point.

Becoming a supernatural leadership wineskin requires that we flow in heavenly grace.

In natural leadership we can only walk in a limited amount of grace, because we need people to behave in predetermined ways or our plans for success could be in jeopardy. If we give people too much latitude, we could possibly lose control of the environment.

The new wineskin of supernatural leadership extends grace generously, because the outcome of our mission is in God's hands. On a practical/spiritual note, a supernatural leader needs to be able to receive grace from others under their leadership in order for there to be freedom. If we want to receive grace, we need to first give it away.

Becoming a supernatural leadership wineskin requires a commitment to lead by doing what is right, not by what is most popular.

This scenario should be more the exception than the rule, but occasionally supernatural leaders will find themselves at this crossroad. Every effort should be made to give those you are leading an opportunity to come with you on your journey toward theocracy. The supernatural leader should always include others by explaining the journey toward a leadership decision, and by sharing the process that was taken to reach a decision. Walking in openness and honesty is crucial for this wineskin. After weighing out your options before the Father and those that are on your team, proceed in humility to do what is on your heart to do.

Becoming a supernatural leadership wineskin requires the inclusion of others in your life that are gifted differently than you.

When our congregation in Minnesota experienced an outpouring of the kingdom, I was blessed to have people around me with differing ministry gifts. The prophetic people spoke into my life concerning what they were hearing and seeing in the Spirit realm. The evangelists kept us focused on the lost. The hospitality people kept the need for service in front of me. The intercessory prayer people kept the role of prayer and fasting on my radar.

I needed all of them and many others that I am failing to mention. Supernatural leaders will not be able to facilitate the leading and development of the church on their own. I believe that God is done with the "one man show." He is wanting us to bring together the various giftings into a team. We must develop, release, and most of all, trust those that are on our team.

Becoming a supernatural leadership wineskin requires that the leader is in a position to be held accountable by others.

From some angles, supernatural leadership can look like a model that encourages leaders to do what they want without accountability. That is a very erroneous conclusion. In fact, due to the nature of the process by which supernatural leaders get their direction for their leadership journey, it necessitates accountability.

A supernatural theocratic leadership is very subjective. Subjectivity allows for a wide variety of ideas and inspirations to be given license to be actively expressed. Just because we are inspired, it doesn't mean that it came from the throne room. All supernatural leaders need a team of people with whom they process what they believe God is saying. Not everything needs to be run by others. How will you learn where those boundaries are? If you have a team of people who are safe with you and are free to express themselves, they will tell you when they should have been consulted. Over time your team will also share with you the things you don't need to bring to them. It will come with "Thanks for giving us a chance to process what you sense that God is saying, but you don't need to include us in this kind of issue in the future."

This team should also have the type of relationship with the supernatural leader in which they can hold the leader accountable for their behavior. We are all at our best when we know that someone is watching. There have been way too many ministries and churches destroyed by leaders who have been living with ungodly character. I am referring to more than immorality. Supernatural leaders that live as new wineskins must be accountable for their attitudes, speech, priorities, spending habits, and fruit.

Becoming a supernatural leadership wineskin requires a regular attendance at the School of the Holy Spirit.

> As for you, the anointing which you received from Him abides in you, and you have no need for anyone to teach you; but as His anointing teaches you about all things, and is true and is not a lie, and just as it has taught you, you abide in Him.
>
> —1 John 2:27

We already have gleaned much from those that have taught us natural leadership. Now it is time to let the Holy Spirit transform us into supernatural leaders. This can only be accomplished by regularly setting time aside to meet with Him.

During your time at the Holy Spirit School you will be:

Reading the Word

There is so much revelation in the Scripture that He will want to show you. He will show you things in verses you have read a number of times over, but never saw. There is a reason why books have been written like *The Da Vinci Code*. For years people have tried to find hidden messages in the Scriptures. In the process they have come up with some very interesting theories. The truth of the matter is that there really are hidden messages in the Scriptures. They have been hidden by the Holy Spirit, for those to whom He wants to bring that revelation. People like you need to receive that revelation, to bless and assist the rest of the body of Christ.

It would be easy for a supernatural leader to focus on the

experience of relationship with the Father and neglect the need for disciplined personal study of the Word. Supernatural leaders who don't maintain a consistent and growing knowledge of the Word are setting themselves up for easy deception. It was not a word or revelation from the Father that empowered Jesus to have victory in a face-to-face with Satan in the wilderness. It was His knowledge of the Word. Any attempt to shortcut your development into a supernatural leader by not regularly reading and studying the Word will set you up for defeat. It is a must. This is one class that you can't cut and get away with it.

Asking Him questions
God rarely answers questions that He has not been asked. Lay out before Him questions that you have concerning direction, vision, relationships, and any area that you lack understanding in.

Listening for His response

> When he puts forth all his own, he goes ahead of them,
> and the sheep follow him because they know his voice.
> —John 10:4

If you are not accustomed to listening to Him talk to you, you are about to begin a wonderful journey. Mark and Patti Virkler's book *How to Hear God's Voice* is a must-read for you.[1] Listen for Him to talk to you at all hours of the day and night. It will be helpful if you keep a journal of the things you hear Him say.

Following what the Spirit deposits into your heart
When you have an inner orientation to move in a specific direction, prayerfully step out in faith. The Holy Spirit is both your guide and helper.

A person of worship
Supernatural leaders are worshipers because it is in worship that everything comes into perspective. In worship we affirm

His power, greatness, provision, and our position in Him. Also, it is in worship that revelation or what some call "downloads" come. When we open up our hearts in worship, He can begin to show us what He is doing.

Supernatural Leaders Are in a Place of Great Responsibility

It is no great revelation to you that leaders are meant to lead the way. John the Baptist had this understanding when he declared that he was the fulfillment of the prophet Isaiah's words:

> "I am a voice of one crying in the wilderness, 'Make straight the way of the Lord,' as Isaiah the prophet said."
>
> —John 1:23

Supernatural leaders are called to remove obstacles that would make it difficult for His presence to come. This is birthed out of our knowledge that what we need most in our ministry is not good training, beautiful buildings, or well-maintained ministry systems. What we need is Him. As Jesus demonstrated in His relationship with Mary and Martha, He loves to come to a place where there has been preparation made for Him.

Pastors and other church leaders serve as spiritual "valves." In other words, what we allow to be "opened up" flows and what we "hold up" is hindered. You know that we have been entrusted with the authority of scripture. When we stand on that authority, things begin to happen.

> "Truly I say to you, whatever you bind on earth shall have been bound in heaven; and whatever you loose on earth shall have been loosed in heaven."
>
> —Matthew 18:18

For a flow and release of the supernatural kingdom in our ministry, we who are in leadership must bless it to be released.

- If a leader is resistant to spontaneity, the Holy Spirit will not be free to flow.

- If a leader has to always control everything, the Holy Spirit will not be free to flow.

- If a leader isn't secure in who they are in Christ, the Holy Spirit will not be free to flow.

- If a leader isn't desirous of supernatural power in their ministry, the Holy Spirit will not be free to flow.

The last time I checked the Word, it looked pretty certain that I am only going to have one chance at life on earth. There will be no second, third, or fourth opportunity to get it right. You are going to have to choose from the same options that were laid out before me. Am I going to take the risks and go after life's possibilities, or am I going to be satisfied with the status quo? Am I going to allow tradition or the expectations of others to determine how high I fly? Am I going to surrender the only life I have to live as a leader to the control of others, or will I walk in freedom to follow what Father God is doing, which is always incredible?

There is nothing like being free to completely follow Him. This is where anything can happen!

PART III:
SUPERNATURAL LEADERSHIP UP FOR DISPLAY

Chapter 9
CONCERNED ABOUT
MY NEW PICTURE?

A T THIS POINT most of you reading this book will have fallen into one of three camps:

- ■ "This resonates with me and is exactly what I have been looking for."

- ■ "I see where you are coming from, but I'm not ready to buy in."

- ■ "I don't agree with you."

This chapter is dedicated to those of you who fall into categories 2 or 3. What some of you have been wrestling with through this journey of considering supernatural leadership is that you keep seeing the "downside." I'm not sure if you are wired like me as a public speaker, but very often when I am presenting a truth that challenges the listener, I start hearing in my spirit many of the "Yes, buts..." "Yes, buts" aren't a bad thing at all. In fact, they help us to look at things from different angles. That is why we are going to look at a number of the "Yes, buts" that have risen up inside of you. I probably will not cover every one that you may have come up with, but I am covering the ones that I personally asked of supernatural leadership over this transitional journey. You will find this chapter helpful as you press toward deciding if supernatural leadership is for you.

Yes, but won't supernatural leadership empower or create a bunch of leadership "mavericks"?

First of all, let's get everyone on the same page by defining a "maverick." The dictionary says that it is "one who refuses adherence to a group." I'm going to take it a step further to add that culturally when most of us hear the term, we think of it in terms of a person who chooses their own path and sometimes rebuffs accountability.

With those definitions in mind, I have to agree that the potential for leadership mavericks does exist. Anytime you turn something imperfect loose, you run the risk of having that imperfection exposed. Since supernatural leadership is being carried through imperfect vessels, it will never be perfect. I also agree with those of you who may be thinking about how a maverick could potentially cause harm in the body of Christ. So, why could taking that kind of risk be a good thing? Well, let's step back for a moment to see what natural leadership has done for us. It has stifled freedom, consumed our energy, put a lid on our possibilities, and taught us to take from others to meet our goals. Not to mention the sleepless nights, tears in the parsonage, ulcers, high blood pressure, prodigal children, and personal unhappiness.

I contend here that for pastors and churches who will step into theocracy and supernatural leadership, there will be less harm done than with natural leadership. Due to the investment into their relationship with Father God, instead of priority being given to building systems and structures, the supernatural leader will walk in greater character. I am also convinced that the supernatural leader will see lasting fruit that has the potential for much greater community impact. Will there be those who will use supernatural leadership as a license to always get their way? Absolutely. A few leaders have always found a way to do that, and sadly, they always will.

Yes but, won't a freed supernatural leader be able to hurt and abuse people without accountability?

Actually, I believe that the answer to this concern is one of the beautiful strengths of supernatural leadership. You see, supernatural leadership isn't just about setting leaders free, it is about setting those under their leadership free as well. Across the United States and around the world, there are countless believers sitting under leadership they don't like, don't agree with, or have concerns about. Why do most of them stay in that environment? Because they are basically committed to the institution of the local church. Obviously, to some extent that can be a good and admirable thing. On the other hand, what the structure of the current church environment has done is encourage a system that keeps people around ineffective leaders in the name of preserving the institution.

The real-life process of supernatural leadership allows the body of Christ opportunity to filter out the leader who doesn't have godly character, or should be pursuing another occupation. Leaders who want to wear the label of supernatural leader, but don't want to develop the character that goes along with it, will over time find themselves without a following.

Yes, but won't supernatural leaders breed or give license to laziness?

In reality, supernatural leadership will demand a high level of self-discipline. As you have seen, one of the greatest disciplines is going to be committing regular, uninterrupted time with Father God. It wouldn't be wise for me to suggest how much time will be needed, but it will need to be a lot and often. Also, if you are thinking that with supernatural leadership there won't be much to do, you are sadly mistaken. After spending time with the Father, Jesus always seemed to have plenty to do. Understand that you will still have some systems and structures that you will need to work with.

A byproduct of supernatural leadership is being at rest and at peace. Just because a leader is at rest and at peace in his or her spirit, it doesn't mean that he or she is lazy. When I have talked about Jesus demonstrating "flow," you may have envisioned a laid-back lifestyle. You are right in the sense that flow comes from a relaxed spirit, but it has nothing to do with the person's work ethic.

Yes, but if natural leadership isn't God's process then why has the church been able to realize the measure of success that it has over the generations?

When I asked this question, the answer came to me at 3:00 a.m. when Nina and I were staying for a few days at the home of a friend. I woke up thinking about this, and here is what I received.

First, I heard Him say to me, "He is a Friend that sticks closer than a brother." Of course this comes from Proverbs:

> A man of too many friends comes to ruin, But there is
> a friend who sticks closer than a brother.
> —Proverbs 18:24

As I pondered it, He began to give understanding. A brother or sister in the natural is someone that you can't choose and can't do much to change that relationship. Since we can't change it, there isn't a high level of motivation to invest into our brothers and sisters. On the other hand, friends are quite optional. I can gain them and I can lose them. In order to maintain a healthy friendship, there are things that we will need to do along the relational journey.

Let me illustrate it to you this way. My best friend's name is Joel. We were visiting the home of Joel and his wife, Roxann, when I received this revelation. While visiting them, let's say that I get up in the morning and think to myself, "I want to go to the stadium and watch a ball game with Joel today." After breakfast, Joel says, "Max, let's go take some parts I have been working on to a customer in the cities. After that we can stop by Home Depot, then come back home to fix my patio." As a person who wants to honor and spend time with my best friend, what would I do? I would go with him wherever he went that day, even though I had a different plan in mind. And, I wouldn't grumble or pout. I would help him to the best of my ability, and just be glad to be with my friend.

This is the picture of Christ's relationship with the church. He is a friend to the church. A very *good* friend. He is someone who had a plan for what He wanted to do with His friend, the church. When the church decided to go its own way and abandon theocracy, He had a choice to make. Because He loves His church, He decided to go with us while we do what we want to do. Since we have seen His uncomplaining hand help the church throughout the years, we have mistakenly told ourselves that what we are doing is and has been what He wants. We have been in error. He has been a friend to His church that has stuck closer than a brother because of love. What a God!

All I am asking us to do now after all of these generations, is to be an honoring friend in return. Is it too much for us to take the risk of looking into His face and saying, "We've done what we wanted to do? Tell me. What do you want to do from here on out?"

You may be asking, "But is it biblical that God would go along with something that wasn't His plan? Consider this passage:

> He said to them, "Because of your hardness of heart Moses permitted you to divorce your wives; but from the beginning it has not been this way."
> —MATTHEW 19:8

Jesus makes it clear here that the position Moses took on divorce was not representative of the Father's will. Yet in context we see that it was not held against Moses. The clear picture on this passage is that God has *gone along* with what Moses established, even though it wasn't representative of kingdom priorities. What we also see represented here as Jesus addresses the topic, is that though the divorce position was tolerated, Jesus is now restoring it back to where it was originally intended to be.

Of course it is our nature to interpret God's blessing or silence as representative of His approval of the paths we choose. His grace, mercy, and love for us do often confuse us when we use them as a measuring device. Perhaps it is time for us to stop measuring and start relating.

Yes, but I've been burned by church leaders. How can I be expected to trust a supernatural leader?

Unfortunately, those of you who relate to that question have a lot of company. A sizeable number of believers in the body of Christ have been wounded by their spiritual leader. Supernatural leadership does require a considerable amount of trust on the part of those who are on the journey with them. Supernatural leaders will be receiving direction through prayer, reading the Word, and wise counsel. They will be listening to hear what the Spirit is saying, and watching to see what the Father is doing. When that revelation is conveyed to the church, those who struggle to trust leaders will potentially struggle to follow.

What is a wounded saint to do when faced with a call to trust a supernatural leader? Probably the first thing that we all need to do is take a deep breath and ask the Holy Spirit to come into these next paragraphs. If you happen to be one of those wounded "hard-to-trust leaders again" saints, my heart goes out to you. For the rest of us who have been blessed to have had leaders who were trustworthy, join me in extending our hands out to this segment of our spiritual family. We need them with us. If you would all extend me the grace, let's walk through the following process together.

1. To those of you who bear the scars and wounds of past church leaders: I humbly ask for your forgiveness on behalf of my peers.

We have at times acted out of our own insecurity and taken it out on you. We have controlled your decisions, demanded that you perform to our standards, missed opportunities when you put your hand out for help, used you to fulfill our desires, verbally beat you up, made you to believe that your value comes from serving us, taught you doctrine that you later found to be untrue, and led you into danger without caring for you. I am so sorry. No excuses. I know that you have never expected perfection, but we should have done better. Will you please forgive us? You never had it coming.

2. To those of you who bear the scars and wounds of past church leaders: now is where you take the first of several difficult steps—forgiveness.

Forgiveness is such an integral part of healthy living that Jesus placed it into the brief prayer that He imparted to the disciples when they asked Him how they should pray.

> Pray, then, in this way: 'Our Father, who is in heaven, Hallowed be Your name. Your kingdom come, Your will be done, On earth as it is in heaven. Give us this day our daily bread. *And forgive us our debts, as we also have forgiven our debtors.* And do not lead us into temptation, but deliver us from evil. [For Yours is the kingdom and the power and the glory forever. Amen.]' *For if you forgive others for their transgressions, your heavenly Father will also forgive you. But if you do not forgive others, then your Father will not forgive your transgressions.*
> —MATTHEW 6:9–15

Forgiveness is so important that after giving the disciples the prayer model, Jesus comes back and reemphasizes its role. Most of you already know that forgiveness is a process, not an event. Rest assured, it was the devil himself who penned the words, "Forgive and forget." Forgetting a situation that caused you pain is not only unrealistic, it often isn't healthy. If we were to forget each painful experience, we would fail to set up the proper boundaries that could prevent it from happening again. Forgiveness at its conclusion will remove the pain and the power of the event to influence your life. That is what your heart is really looking for. Each time the memory of the wound comes to mind, choose to forgive them and let them go. If Jesus expects us to do it, it is, in fact, doable.

3. To those of you who bear the scars and wounds of past church leaders: I ask you to go the next step of the journey and bless those leaders who have brought you hurt.

Yes, you read it right. Bless them. Romans 12:14 states:

> Bless those who persecute you; bless and do not curse.

There is supernatural power in blessing. This is not just an exercise that shifts your thinking. This is an activity that actually changes circumstances and hearts. Blessing has power. The devil knows that you will never be able to rise to your potential with unforgiveness in your heart. He will do all he can to make sure you remember and relive those painful moments. To send a blessing from heaven to the ones who have wounded you each time he reminds you is counterproductive for him. If you will just step out and speak a blessing of God's best, mercy, health, prosperity, freedom, joy, and anything else that rises in your spirit, you will be amazed at how quickly he will stop reminding you of their hurt. Just do your part, and God will do His!

4. To those of you who bare the scars and wounds of past church leaders: repeat numbers 2 and 3, as often as they come to mind.

5. To those of you who bear the scars and wounds of past church leaders: your last step is to get into alignment with a supernatural leader that you feel you can trust.

For some of you, you will choose to line up behind the one who you originally distrusted. I commend you for giving them another chance. For others of you, it will mean that you will need to begin looking for a new leader. As you do, listen and watch potential leaders with your eyes, ears and most importantly your heart. Though we often should be cautious about following our hearts, you will find it to be correct more often than not. Take whatever steps that you feel you need to, in order to be able to discern your potential supernatural leader. Real supernatural leaders will not be put off by your inquiry, and they will appreciate your interest in the potential relationship.

Once you have gotten behind a supernatural leader, you are now ready to begin taking risks again. Give them some rope to see what they do with it. When we give people some rope—freedom to move—they will do one of two things with it. They will either use it constructively and make good things happen with it, or they will hang themselves with it. Give your leader some chances to see what they will do. Though they will never be able to live up to perfection, if your leader shows the evidence of good fruit out of challenging situations, they should be allowed to earn your trust. Actually, I think that you will enjoy the journey!

Yes, but under supernatural leadership, won't the church move into disorder and chaos?

We have become so secure in how we do church, that the thought that it could be done differently can be somewhat unsettling. One of the things that may be unsettling for many of you is that I have not clearly outlined what a supernaturally led church would look like. Why? Because for me to do that, it would tempt you to try to take my template and make it work in your situation. Theocracy as it is worked out through supernatural leadership, doesn't have a "one size fits all" template.

Rest in knowing that He is not a God of chaos and disorder. Let's also be realistic in agreeing that what is chaotic or out of order is subjective to our personal experience. Yes, there will need to be a season of transition for all leaders and churches that want to move into theocracy and supernatural leadership. It will not be an overnight or perfect process. Yes, supernatural leadership can potentially change the church as we know it. My heart and prayer is that I hope it does!

Yes, but supernatural leadership sounds very experienced-based. I've always been taught not to trust experiences.

You're right, supernatural leadership does lean on experiences. Supernatural leadership is based on relationship. That relationship is between the leader and Father God. The interesting thing about a relationship is this: try having one without any experiences. Try having a relationship with your children without any experiences together. Try having a relationship with your best friend without experiencing anything between you. Relationships must be experienced. Without it, all you have is head knowledge about a person or topic.

Living in the supernatural is living in experience. If all you want to do with your ministry is pass out information that you have gotten from someone else, have at it. That's what has been happening for generations in all kinds of churches around the world. Like Dr. Phil says to his television guests, "So how is that working for you?"

Yes, but supernatural leadership doesn't sound very democratic.

You know, that's an interesting dynamic that the U. S. church has to deal with. We love and are proud of our national democracy and our representative government. Voting on people that we choose to represent us on policy issues is the basis of how we function. As a culture and nation it not only has served us well, but whenever possible, we try to help other nations develop a similar model. So, since God has helped us and blessed us as a nation with a representative government, what is good for this country must be good for the church. (Now, haven't we heard that rationale somewhere before?) As a result, many have set up their churches with elected pastors and elected boards. Yes, it does work to some extent, but the church wasn't meant to be set up with a representative government, it was supposed to be a theocracy.

In a theocracy, supernatural leaders are free to guide the churches as they see the Father guiding them. You may be wondering if it would be possible to combine the two. In other words, can you have a supernatural leader in a representative governed church? I think that there is potential for there to be some level of success with that scenario. The blending of the two models will pose some challenges, but it could potentially work if one particular dynamic remains constant. That dynamic is that the pastor must remain "free." When the pastor is unable to be free to walk out supernatural leadership, it will become an unhealthy situation.

Again, remember that God being in charge and leading through His chosen representative is His best plan. We've tried for three thousand years to do better and have failed. Should we just keep on trying?

Yes, but I'm too old to move into a new type of leadership.

Believe me, I understand your heart, but it's just not the truth. The Bible says:

> But no one puts a patch of unshrunk cloth on an old garment; for the patch pulls away from the garment, and a worse tear results.
>
> —MATTHEW 9:16

There is a place for older and experienced patches. Supernatural leadership needs people to step in who have had years to develop and mature. I know that culturally, a lot of responsibility and authority is being given to the younger generation. On the other hand, I am convinced that if those who have years of life experience under their belt don't stay in the race, we are handicapping those who are younger. The local church needs the mature leaders. Personally, it is going to be a long time before I pass off the baton in my hand to a younger runner. I'm in this thing to cross the finish line.

Supernatural leadership is not a giant leap. It is already in you, which makes it very doable. Your only significant challenge will be to stay focused on supernatural living. If you don't, you will fall back into natural institutional thinking. I believe that supernatural leadership is your leadership destiny.

Chapter 10
TAKE THE PICTURE HOME

T HERE IS A lot to be said for experience. If you will allow the experiences of your life to be filed for future reference, a thick file can be very beneficial. Here is a lesson from one of the files Nina and I keep—our "shopping experience" file. While browsing a store we would come across an item that we had on our *someday* list, at a drastic price reduction. Standing before the display, we would talk about the value of the deal and whether or not we could afford it. Invariably, we would always reach the same decision: "We'll get it the next time we come." On the drive home, we would discuss it some more, often with the conclusion, "We should have picked it up." Dutifully, in one or two weeks we visited that store again, we would remind ourselves to pick up the item. With anticipation and expectation we would make our way over to where the display had been. Invariably every time we did this, we found the item was no longer available. Not only did we not get the item that we wanted, but we would end up paying substantially more for a similar item at a later date. Experience has caused us to change how we respond to an unexpected bargain. When we're willing to pay the price and it's exactly what we are looking for, we take it home with us.

For each of you who have been standing in front of the supernatural leadership display of the previous chapters, it is about time to make some lasting decisions. I've been painting a new leadership picture for you, and in this chapter I will add the finishing touches. Will you take it home or leave it for another day? You'll know what to do. Right now just step back for a moment and allow me to finish getting this ready for you.

A supernatural leader is a community leader.

I am quite confident that your town, city, or region could benefit from a supernatural leader who is willing to get involved with the local community—someone who will get into the trenches with city councils, police departments, fire departments, civic organizations, schools, business owners, and human services. Your area would benefit from someone who will not just complain about how bad things are, but will place himself or herself into arenas that can shape and alter a community's destiny. Supernatural leaders do not focus on condemning the darkness, but allow the Father to direct them to places where they can shine His light of love, affirmation, and hope.

Some of you pastors and church leaders have never really ever seen yourself stepping into the arena of local community. One of the potential reasons for that is that natural leadership has led many of you to believe that you don't have authority or responsibility outside of your system. Natural leadership has a tendency to compartmentalize territory. Another way of putting it is to say that natural leadership has built in limitations as to how far authority can be extended.

Supernatural leaders understand that they are called to influence the community. Their leadership isn't compartmentalized, but functions as a flow out into a culture in complete disorder. America needs to have its communities reclaimed by the kingdom of God. Supernatural leaders will carry the potential to shift whole communities.

You are standing in familiar shoes.

Remember the story of the rich young ruler? You've read it countless times and have perhaps taught or preached about him on a number of occasions. Did you ever foresee the day when you could potentially be standing in his shoes?

> And someone came to Him and said, "Teacher, what good thing shall I do that I may obtain eternal life?" And He said to him, "Why are you asking Me about what is good? There is only One who is good; but if you wish to enter into life, keep the commandments." Then he said to Him, "Which ones?" And Jesus said, "You shall not commit murder; you shall not commit adultery; you shall not steal; you shall not bear false witness; honor your father and mother; and you shall love your neighbor as yourself." The young man said to Him, "All these things I have kept; what am I still lacking?" Jesus said to him, "If you wish to be complete, go and sell your possessions and give to the poor, and you will have treasure in heaven; and come, follow Me." But when the young man heard this statement, he went away grieving; for he was one who owned much property.
>
> —MATTHEW 19:16–22

How can his story and yours coincide? First, he confesses to Jesus that he has done everything that he knew to do. He has made every effort to do his best to be a spiritual success. You may feel that I am being presumptuous, but I have reason to believe that this is also your leadership confession. You have done your best to fulfill your leadership obligations, and you have applied your training toward being an impact leader for God's church. You have built the teams, orchestrated the meetings, set up the structure, and laid out yourself for God's people.

Secondly, his story could be yours because the Bible shows us that after all that he had done, he still had a sense that something was missing:

> "All these things I have kept; what am I still lacking?"
>
> —MATTHEW 19:20

Like the rich young ruler, you have had a revelation of the Holy Spirit. How do I know that? You wouldn't be reading this chapter if you didn't have a sincere hunger to function with leadership in Christ at a different level. That's OK. In fact, it's a good thing. A *really* good thing!

What did Jesus tell him that he needed to do in order to function at a higher level in the kingdom?

> "Go and sell your possessions and give to the poor, and you will have treasure in heaven; and come, follow Me."
> —MATTHEW 19:21

In essence, Jesus is telling this young man that if he really wants to step from meeting the obligations of a system, to living in freedom at a supernatural level, he will need to let go of the systems with which he has identified himself. It is a call to take a risk that doesn't fit in a box and does not meet all of the logical criteria of sound reasoning. This call only fits in the heart.

How many times have we read this passage and thought to ourselves "What a fool! Couldn't he see that what Jesus had to offer was so much bigger than where he had been? Couldn't he see that his heart was leading him to the truth, and that he needed to follow it? Couldn't he see that Jesus was asking him to trade rags for kingdom riches?" We all know that when he walked away from Jesus that day, he made the grandest mistake of his life.

Yet, by the world's standards, what Jesus was asking of him was a very high price. He had the attachment to stuff, financial security, and the praise of man for being such a devoted guy. Jesus was just making it clear up front (something that we don't always handle well). He was communicating to this rich young ruler that if you are going to step into the kingdom arena with Him, it can't be all about you. Is that a fair trade? Of course not! How can you call something fair when you trade what is temporary and consuming for what is eternal, freeing, and life giving? The rich young ruler really had nothing of value to lose and everything of value to gain.

Supernatural leadership will call you to let go of what at times has given you value, security, and identity. What do you get in return? You receive value, security, and identity that come from Him. You get freedom to follow flow, instead of an obligation to meet the demands of systems. For some of you it could be considered a high price to pay. You may think it to be too high of a price to pay, too big of a risk to take, too odd to follow your heart instead of your training.

Was Jesus' request of the rich young ruler unreasonable? It is the question that you will have to answer for your own personal journey. Is stepping into supernatural leadership and leaving behind natural leadership an unreasonable step of obedience?

> But when the young man heard this statement, he went away grieving; for he was one who owned much property.
>
> —MATTHEW 19:22

We know what his choice was, and we know how his heart felt about that choice. How will your heart feel about your choice?

Not everyone will cheer you on or understand you.

If you haven't noticed by now, the ways of God do not always line up with the ways of man. That, of course, is why people who are going to follow Christ are called to a life of faith. We walk this journey out in faith, because much of what we step into has little rational value, such as:

- Trusting a God you can't see
- Giving money away
- Mutual submission
- Humility
- Honesty

Supernatural leadership is a lifestyle that will defy natural and historical reasoning. Either to your face or behind your back, somebody is going to be laughing at you. They will probably come up with original descriptions of you like heretic, fanatic, rebellious, independent and off the deep end. Do you have the picture? To walk in supernatural leadership could potentially make some who are close to you very uncomfortable.

The reasons are two-fold. First, some will be genuinely concerned about you. They love you and want what's best for you. Their concern will be that supernatural leadership isn't the best for you and your career. The second reason you will make others uncomfortable is that your choices will force them to have to evaluate their choices. They could potentially reason that if you are convinced that supernatural leadership is of God, then where does that leave them? Human nature historically doesn't handle this kind of tension very well.

Unfortunately, what often happens is that the person who challenges the status quo becomes the bad guy. Why? Everything was "just fine" until you decided to step out of the box. So, instead of being open to examine themselves, they attack the one who incited an agitation and threatens to mess up their world that they have under "control." As Jesus prepared to perform a miracle, the verse in Matthew 9:24 states:

> He said, "Leave; for the girl has not died, but is asleep."
> And they began laughing at Him.

They laughed at Him. They may very well laugh at you.

> As they were going out, a mute, demon-possessed man was brought to Him. After the demon was cast out, the mute man spoke; and the crowds were amazed, and were saying, "Nothing like this has ever been seen in Israel." But the Pharisees were saying, "He casts out the demons by the ruler of demons."
> —MATTHEW 9:32–34

There will be good fruit coming from your supernatural leadership. People's lives will be changed. They will be healed, freed, restored, and equipped. Even after all of that, the religiously established will say that you are operating out of a wrong spirit. They will try to incite others against you. Please hear what I am about to say. Don't waste your time and energy in pointless debate. Pray for them. Bless them and continue on. To enter into a debate with the intent of changing their minds will inevitably end up with you wounded and frustrated. On the other hand, look for opportunities to share your journey and give an honest account to everyone who is earnestly seeking and interested in what God is doing in your life.

Along with all of the incredible advantages of being a supernatural leader, you will also at times be faced with pain. It's a good pain, because it exists in you due to the fact that you care. If you didn't care about what people who are in relationship with you think, the pain wouldn't be there. You already know that the prize is worth much more than the pain, don't you?

As was illustrated by the rich young ruler's encounter with Jesus, the choices that must be made to follow Him can, at times, be painful. Walking *into* the Spirit's call to higher kingdom living means walking *away* from something else. Some of you will walk away from people in which you have invested so much of your life. Some will walk away from long-time friends. Some will walk away from job security. Some will walk away from their homes. Some will walk away from unfulfilled dreams and visions of what might have been. Some will walk away from environments where prophetic words have yet to be realized. Some will walk away from all I have just mentioned and more. It can be a challenge, and it can be very painful.

So, why subject yourself to such pain? If you choose supernatural leadership, you will choose the potential of pain because you want to live the rest of your life at a higher level of spiritual and ministry effectiveness. You will choose it because to be free from the demands and control of natural leadership is well worth the price. You will choose it because He is calling you to cast down your nets and follow Him. You will take the risks and follow Him. You will take the risks and endure the pain because you have an appointment with your destiny. There is a hurting and dysfunctional world out there that is waiting for supernatural leaders.

I must take you on a side journey for a moment. Some of you need to see what I am about to open up. I think that by now you would agree with me that Jesus was the ultimate supernatural leader. It doesn't get any better than watching the Messiah demonstrate leadership. Let me ask you a few questions. Do the Gospels record that Jesus ever attempted to change the way the synagogue system was set up to address Jewish spirituality? Did He try to change its function? Did He try to change its mission? The answer to all of these questions is "no."

Jesus never really attempted to transform or convert the synagogue system. He honored it with His attendance throughout His lifetime and treated it with respect. So what did He do when He began His ministry after returning from forty days in the wilderness? Did He run to the synagogue to preach good news to the poor, proclaim freedom to captives, sight to the blind, free the oppressed, and proclaim the time was now for the favor of the Lord? We see Jesus simply choose to step out of an established religious structure and system in order to be free to build the kingdom as the Father directed. Many of you who choose to step into supernatural leadership will *not* need to do that. You are already in a place that is ready to transition into supernatural leadership, or at least the foundation is there for its development. Rejoice!

On the other hand, some of you may find that you will need to do what Jesus did. Don't even try to take on the religious system and establishment. Just walk away in honor, in respect, and in anticipation of preaching Good News to the poor, proclaiming freedom to captives, sight to the blind, freeing the oppressed and proclaiming the time is now for the favor of the Lord.

For those of you leaders who are married, use some Christ-like common sense as you walk this out. You are not the only person who will be affected by the significant decisions in life that you are about to make. The journey of supernatural leadership must be walked out with your spouse. Hopefully, he/she has been reading this book with you. If not, give your spouse the opportunity to do so in order to get on the same page with you. Your spouse will need to have the opportunity for personal buy-in concerning supernatural leadership. Buy-in is not the same as force-in. If you are not first a supernatural leader at home, you will never be able to be a fruitful one outside of the home.

Transitioning into supernatural leadership is going to mean change. All change needs to be endorsed with confirmation from your spouse. Mutual submission is a biblical principle that cannot be violated by a personal revelation, good intention, or an inspiring book. This is not a one-person journey. Honor your spouse by freeing and empowering him or her to weigh supernatural leadership for himself or herself. Until your spouse is walking in alignment with you in your leadership, don't attempt the journey. If your spouse is not in favor of affirming you to step into supernatural leadership, use this season to find out why. You may hear some things that will be hard for you to hear, but receive it in grace. Humble yourself. Walk in honor toward your spouse, and prayerfully seek for His resolution to your particular situation. True unity and agreement means everything in the kingdom.

There is not one set model for what supernatural leadership should look like.

Some of you are still waiting for me to put together a step-by-step process for supernatural leadership. Others are trying to figure out what this will look like on a flow chart. I am afraid that you have an expectation that I won't be able to fulfill. You see, if you take supernatural leadership and attempt to place it into a model, you take the risk of setting it up as another system. You don't need to be trading one system for another. However, I can remind you of the significant components of supernatural leadership that I believe must be brought into place as you walk the journey:

- Spend regular time with Father God.

- Learn to know His voice.

- Learn to see things with your spiritual eyes.

- Read His Word and stay tuned in for Holy Spirit revelation.

- Walk in brokenness and humility.

- Give God chances to do the impossible.

- Allow others to hold you accountable.

The beauty of supernatural leadership is that it can be lived out in any house church, independent, or denominational setting as long as the supernatural leader has the freedom to follow the Father's direction. Supernatural leadership is not a Western or American form of leadership. It is kingdom of God leadership. It's a theocracy of God choosing to lead His people through someone of His choice, who will follow what they see in the kingdom and hear in the Spirit. Since it is kingdom of God leadership, it also transcends every ethnic and cultural barrier. Theocracy was God's plan for all of His people, so it will work with "every tribe and every tongue."

As a new wine skin, the intent of supernatural leadership is to be able to carry the new outpouring of the kingdom of God with longevity. When His presence and power step into our environment, our desire is that this occurrence will not just be a historical moment in time. We want His presence to shift the atmosphere indefinitely and that individuals, families, businesses, territories and governments will be transformed. Can you or I do that? That's the point. We've been failing at if for thousands of years. Can He do that through our leadership and those that we lead? Absolutely. That has always been His plan.

For all of you reading this book that are not called to lead, there are a few things that you will need to remember in order to support and follow a supernatural leader.

If you are serving under a pastor or spiritual leader who is pursuing the journey to become a supernatural leader, you need to go through a season of releasing him/her. You may have accumulated a number of expectations through the years of relationship. Those expectations can, at times, serve as emotional strings that you pull on whenever you have some type of personal need. Even though your pastor/spiritual leader doesn't know where the pull is coming from, he or she can feel it in his or her spirit. The greater the number of people with those strings of expectations, the greater the bondage is on the heart of your leader. A supernatural leader has to be free of these strings, free to pursue the kingdom. Does this mean that you don't ever talk with your pastor about what you need or what you are going through? Absolutely not! He/she loves you, cares about you, and wants to serve you by bringing the kingdom into your situation.

Set them free from historic systems and structures that have consumed so much of their time and energy. Set them free from any environment where you or others have been in a place of "managing" their ministry. That is the tail wagging the dog. It was never meant to be that way. People do not manage the kingdom. God does. It will make for a happier dog and tail.

Stay in prayer for your pastor as he/she steps into supernatural leadership. Pray for them in these ways:

- To receive Holy Spirit revelation

- To have passion and courage

- To have simple, childlike faith

- That the assignments of the enemy would fail

- That supernatural provision of heaven would be theirs as a testimony of God's goodness toward His own

- That the wisdom of God would be established in their hearts

- As a watchman on the wall, to protect them from those who would do them harm

If you have the honor and privilege of serving under a supernatural leader as he or she walks through the process of shifting a ministry from natural leadership, I want to affirm you. I affirm you to commit yourself both to your leader and to the process.

Transitioning an established ministry from natural leadership to supernatural leadership is like living in an old house while you are remodeling it. Remodeling is very messy. Through the process, there are differences of opinion about what should be done, the color of the paint, choice of floor coverings, fixtures, and the costs. Furniture has to be shifted from room to room. Dirt and dust are everywhere. Normal schedules are disrupted, and it at times it is very noisy. All of this can also be found in transitioning a ministry from natural leadership to supernatural leadership. Your supernatural leader will need people who will be willing to help with any messes that may arise.

In a home remodeling project, you have to keep your eye on the goal and remind yourself in the midst of the mess that it will all be worth it when you're done. The same can be true for churches and ministries. Should things get messy, put your eyes on the prize. Just imagine the joy of giving the Good News to the poor, freedom to the captives, sight to the blind, freeing the oppressed, and proclaiming that now is the time for the favor of the Lord!

Fulfilling the requirements that natural leadership and religion demand does bring a certain level of satisfaction. But as the rich young ruler points out by his inquiry of Jesus, there is still a sense that something big is missing. Don't let the process and potential mess of letting go of natural leadership keep you from stepping into the realm of the kingdom of God where the supernatural is the new normal. Let me assure you that I have spied out the land that flows with milk and honey. Yes, there are some giants in the land, but God is just waiting for some Joshuas to take them down and repossess the land. The fruit there is incredible!

CONCLUSION

After everything that we have been through in the previous chapters, I want to draw it all together with some insight into Moses, who was one of God's great—but not perfect—theocratic leaders.

When it comes to reflecting on Moses' defining leadership moments, what many of us remember is the account of the moment in time that his actions cost him the privilege of going into the Promised Land.

> "Take the rod; and you and your brother Aaron assemble the congregation and speak to the rock before their eyes, that it may yield its water. You shall thus bring forth water for them out of the rock and let the congregation and their beasts drink." So Moses took the rod from before the LORD, just as He had commanded him; and Moses and Aaron gathered the assembly before the rock. And he said to them, "Listen now, you rebels; shall we bring forth water for you out of this rock?" Then Moses lifted up his hand and struck the rock twice with his rod; and water came forth abundantly, and the congregation and their beasts drank. But the LORD said to Moses and Aaron, "Because you have not believed Me, to treat Me as holy in the sight of the sons of Israel, therefore you shall not bring this assembly into the land which I have given them."
>
> —Numbers 20:8–12

There are a number of different angles from which we can look at this event. What I see here is a leader who let those that he is leading get under his skin. Out of his anger toward the people, he hits the rock instead of speaking to it. His hurt and frustration have superseded the simple direction from heaven. The price that Moses pays for this act of disobedience, should remind us all of the priority that God places on obedience with His supernatural leaders. Though this Moses leadership moment is one that we all recall, I want to bring you to another one that reveals a different side of Moses.

Numbers 14 records a season of leadership for Moses. Israel has just listened to the reports of the spies who have returned from the Promised Land. Joshua and Caleb have delivered their report along with the other spies, and the people are beginning to respond.

> Then all the congregation lifted up their voices and cried, and the people wept that night. All the sons of Israel grumbled against Moses and Aaron; and the whole congregation said to them, "Would that we had died in the land of Egypt! Or would that we had died in this wilderness! Why is the LORD bringing us into this land, to fall by the sword? Our wives and our little ones will become plunder; would it not be better for us to return to Egypt?" So they said to one another, "Let us appoint a leader and return to Egypt."
> —NUMBERS 14:1–4

In response to such outcry, Moses and Aaron fall on their faces and implore the people of Israel not to reject the report of Joshua and Caleb. They exhorted the people to believe that their God is bigger than the giants in the Promised Land.

> But all the congregation said to stone them with stones. Then the glory of the LORD appeared in the tent of meeting to all the sons of Israel. The LORD said to

Moses, "How long will this people spurn Me? And how long will they not believe in Me, despite all the signs with I have performed in their midst? I will smite them with pestilence and dispossess them, and I will make you into a nation greater and mightier than they."

—Numbers 14:10–12

God's presence appears to Moses, and He is not happy with Israel's rejection of His plan and provision. He tells Moses of what He will do because of Israel's rejection of Him. The description is twofold. First, He is going to kill them all off. Secondly, He tells Moses that He will make for him a nation of people greater than Israel.

Did you catch that? Moses heard God tell him on one hand of His displeasure with others, and on the other hand He is so pleased with Moses that He wants to make him mightier. To paraphrase it, what Moses heard was this: "Moses, you're the man! I'm going to kill off everyone who is rebelling against your leadership, and give you a big promotion." Honestly, how many of us that have any history in trying to lead God's people, wouldn't jump on an offer like that one?

Moses' response to God's offer is incredible.

But Moses said to the Lord, "Then the Egyptians will hear of it, for by Your strength You brought up this people from their midst, and they will tell it to the inhabitants of this land. They have heard that You, O Lord, are in the midst of this people, for You, O Lord, are seen eye to eye, while Your cloud stands over them; and You go before them in a pillar of cloud by day and in a pillar of fire by night. Now if You slay this people as one man, then the nations who have heard of Your fame will say, "Because the Lord could not bring this people into the land which He promised them by oath, therefore He slaughtered them in the wilderness." But

now, I pray, let the power of the Lord be great, just as
You have declared.

—NUMBERS 14:13–17

Moses' response in these verses and those following was
expressed in a remarkable manner. Let me again paraphrase
what Moses tells God: "Don't do it, God! Don't punish these
that are complaining about you and about my leadership (even
though they are trying to find my replacement.) Don't make
me powerful and prosperous at their expense. This isn't about
me. This is all about you and what is best for your kingdom."
His response almost brings me to tears every time I consider
it. Moses wasn't in supernatural leadership for himself. Moses
accepted God's call to supernatural leadership—not for what he
could gain, but for what others could gain by encountering the
living God through him.

This was a defining moment for Moses.

What will you now do with your defining moment?

NOTES

Chapter 1
We're in This Together

1. Oswald Sanders, *Spiritual Leadership* (Chicago, IL: Moody Press, 1994), 52, 71, 118, 127, 138.

2. Bill Hybels, *Courageous Leadership* (Grand Rapids, MI: Zondervan, 2002), 37, 71, 46, 80, 141,

3. Andy Stanley, *Next Generation Leader* (Sisters, OR: Multnomah, 2003), 11–12.

4. John Maxwell, *The 21 Most Powerful Minutes in a Leaders Day* (Nashville, TN: Thomas Nelson, 2000), v–viii.

5. Chris Brady and Orrin Woodward, *Launching a Leadership Revolution* (Grand Blanc, MI: Obstacle Press, 2006), 127, 154, 185, 207, 256.

Chapter 8
Creating a New Image

1. Mark Virkler and Patti Virkler, *How to Hear God's Voice* (Shippensburg, PA: Destiny Image Publishers, 2006).

■ ■ ■

To Contact the Author
max@verticalleadership.net

■ ■ ■